HIGH IMPACT
TELEPHONE
NETWORKING
_{FOR} JOB HUNTERS

Who to call

What to say

How to project a positive image

How to turn contacts into job offers

Howard Armstrong

BOB ADAMS, INC.
PUBLISHERS
Holbrook, Massachusetts

Published by Bob Adams, Inc.
260 Center Street, Holbrook, MA 02343

Manufactured in the United States of America.

ISBN: 1-55850-114-2

A B C D E F G H I J

COVER PHOTO: FPG International, M. Simpson

DEDICATION

To my father, Dick Lutz,
and my mother-in-law, Alberta Kirkpatrick.
Their help through tough times has assured that
Howard Armstrong Associates, Inc. has survived
the worst possible time to start a business.

TABLE OF CONTENTS

". . . over 90 percent of what we worry about never really happens. In other words, our fears, worries, and apprehensions have less than one chance in ten of becoming a reality." (Susan Jeffers, Ph.D.)

The hiring process is anything but an exact science. Personal chemistry is more important to the hiring decision than most people are willing to admit. An appointment with a network contact can establish this chemistry.

This chapter describes a simple, 6-step process that will generate all the contacts you can handle. The remaining chapters describe the finer points of each step in the process.

ACKNOWLEDGMENTS

The first order of business is to recognize the seminar participants whose frank, honest, and creative contributions provided a great deal of the material for this book. One participant who stands out in my mind is Cliff Stark, who proved that some very good things can emerge from a disastrous situation.

Special thanks go to a very special friend who wrote *AFTER COLLEGE: The Business of Getting Jobs, What's Next? Career Strategies After 35*, and *The absolute very best of Jack Falvey*, Jack Falvey. Jack's love of God and sincere desire to help others succeed is evident in every "back porch" conversation we have. Thanks Jack!

This book would still be sitting on the shelf were it not for Joan Koob Cannie, author of *Keeping Customers for Life*. One day, while working with her on a newsletter, she said to me, "If there's one piece of advice I can give you, it's to write a book!"

Also, a very special word of thanks to my friend, pastor, and editor, Howard "Skip" MacMullen. Skip's unselfish provision of time and talent is especially appreciated in assisting me to complete this work, considering the tight deadlines he was given to work with.

And finally, to Amy, Sean, and Abby, I give my thanks and love for the many hours I spent with this book and not with them.

INTRODUCTION

You should read this book if you . . .

- are out of work as a result of a lay-off, down-sizing, reorganization, or reduction in force (RIF).
- have been fired.
- have been selected for outplacement.
- are currently employed but are seriously considering a career change (for whatever reason).
- think you have run out of contacts.
- dislike the idea of "networking," because it means *making telephone calls!*
- think networking sounds too much like selling.
- have sent out dozens (nay, hundreds!) of cover letters and resumes, without much to show for your efforts.
- feel stagnated in your career search.
- fear that the job market is "saturated" with people in your specialty.
- would like a career search system that will yield a return on your time investment that is directly proportional to your efforts.

- ❑ would like a method that provides immediate feed-back on its effectiveness.

- ❑ would like a process that may reduce the time it takes to find the right opportunity by up to 75 percent.

❑   ❑   ❑

A man from Boston walked into my office one day and said, "Howard, there is no way anyone is going to hire me at my age! I'm 57 years old."

I said, "Oh?"

He said, "Well, it's not just my age. I've been a Director of Human Resources in the finance industry for over 15 years. The industry is saturated with people like me. They don't need me. And even if there was an opening in my field, it would probably be far away, and my wife and I would have to relocate. In any case, I don't think there is much hope for my situation."

I thought for a moment and said, "Well, there's one thing I can promise you . . . if that's what you honestly believe, that's exactly what will happen! If, on the other hand, you are willing to work with me to put a plan together and make a commitment to execute it, you might be pleasantly surprised!"

Approximately six weeks later, he wrote to tell me that he had become the Director of Human Resources for a bank in the Boston area.

Another time, a woman I worked with insisted she could never use the telephone to win appointments, nor could she discuss her career over the telephone. She explained that talking on the telephone was extremely uncomfortable for her. She said, "It just scares me to death, especially in a business setting!"

After discussing specific areas of discomfort, we outlined a plan of action tailored to her personality. The plan included an introductory statement that she felt comfortable with. We also anticipated the typical questions that she might be asked. And I challenged her to get the names of at least two more contacts from each person she spoke to.

One week later, she returned to my office with good news. "I called a man to set an appointment exactly the way we had planned it." When she got to the point where she was supposed to get the names of two others to call, her contact said, "Are you kidding! The way you sound, I wouldn't give your name to anyone until I've met you first myself!"

❑   ❑   ❑

As a corporate trainer, I have been "outplaced" twice and fired once. At one point during these difficult situations, I actually owned three homes. To say that I needed to do something fast is an understatement!

During those jobless days, I learned that the best friend we have is God, and the best tool he gave us is the telephone.

Using the process I describe in this book, I found a training management position at the same salary my previous employer paid, and I did it in just six weeks after being fired! Think about that. If I had left of my own accord (which I did not) and subsequently found a similar position at roughly the same salary in three to six *months*, that would have been about par for the course. However, I didn't leave voluntarily. I had been *fired* (something about "not fitting the corporate mold," whatever that means).

In professional career counseling circles, locating a similar position at the same salary in just six weeks after termination was unheard of! Yet there was no magic. You see, one of the first things I realized is that much of the stigma associated with "being fired" is one we place upon ourselves. I simply made up my mind that being fired was actually *their* loss and not mine. I began using what I call the two basic ground rules of high impact telephone networking. I describe both the process and ground rules in the chapters that follow.

I think it's fair to say I am living proof that effective telephone networking can dramatically reduce the time it takes to find the right career opportunity.

Now, you may be thinking, "This sort of thing is perfect . . . for a salesperson. After all, they make their living talking on the telephone, because they're good at it. They have the personality to 'pull it off.' *I* could never do that!" Well, I'll let you in on a little secret. The success that people have enjoyed from my telephone networking seminars is due in large part to the fact that this material is geared toward the *non-selling individual*!

My promise to you is this. If you use the techniques, guidelines, and check lists in this book, you will dramatically reduce the time it takes you to find the right career—for one very simple reason. It takes far less time to make a telephone call than to write a letter, put it in the mail, and then wait for corporation to take the necessary steps to respond.

In this process, you will contact those *who know the people* who can offer you the position you want. (As you probably already know, asking a stranger *for a job* over the phone directly is likely to lead to disappointment. My bet is that *that's* what most people dread—and fortunately, it's not part of my system.) The telephone is the fastest and most efficient way to make this happen. Jack Falvey, the author of *What's Next? Career Strategies After 35*, offers this challenge in favor of networking over broadcast cover letters and resumes. He says, "You don't want to look good on paper. You want to be good in person."

This process can put you in front of the people who can make it happen for you. But quit stalling. Every minute you waste deciding if reading this book would be a good investment of your time is just one more minute that is keeping me from proving to you that the system works!

CHAPTER 1

THE TELEPHONE: WHY WE DON'T USE IT.

Over the past few years, I have given many High Impact Telephone Networking seminars to help people expedite the process of finding new career opportunities through the use of the telephone.

The first exercise of the program is to divide the participants into teams to discuss the following questions: why we are reluctant to use the telephone when pursuing career opportunities? These small groups discuss the question for about thirty minutes, and then reconvene to report their findings to the rest of the seminar members.

While this exercise naturally results in many different answers, some replies are remarkably similar from meeting to meeting. Here is a sample of the responses consistently generated at these meetings.

> "I'm *afraid* I won't be able to carry on an intelligent conversation, because I will be so *nervous* that I won't know what to say."

> "I just don't like talking on the telephone."

> "I feel I have a better chance of impressing someone with a well thought-out cover letter than simply

trying to call and convince someone that I am worth talking to."

"I *fear* rejection."

"I have a *fear* of knocking myself out of contention by saying the wrong thing, instead of letting my resume do the talking."

"It *bothers* me when I am talking to someone and cannot see [the contact's] body language or facial expressions."

"Whenever I start talking to someone about networking over the telephone, I get the impression that he is rolling his eyes in disgust, as if he can't wait for this call to end."

"I'm afraid of making a friend look bad (when following up on a referral), due to my poor performance over the telephone."

"I'm *afraid* they (telephone contact) will equate future performance with telephone prowess."

"I feel like somebody standing on a street corner with a tin cup in my hand and begging for work."

"There's something about the telephone that *scares me*."

This is just a sample of what I usually hear. However, there is a common thread running through these responses. Notice how the statements include words like "afraid," "worried," "concerned," and "fear." In other words, the thought of using the phone to pursue career opportunities is uncomfortable to them. Perhaps they imagine danger or some bad past experience is about to befall them.

This brings to mind a statement that is especially appropriate here and is one I will always remember. It comes from Ed Foreman, a colleague in the National Speaker's Association. He is also the only American in the last century to have held seats in the House of Representatives from two different states (Texas and New Mexico). In regard to fear, Foreman states: "Worry is nothing more than the misuse of our imagination. It is thinking vividly about what we do not want to see happen in the future, or dwelling on an undesirable past event."

Think about this statement and apply it to the seminar participants' responses above. Despite the fact that we know the telephone is just about as fast as the speed of light, we fail to take advantage of it because we are afraid. The truth is, we tend to shy away from the telephone. This is not because we are afraid of the equipment, but because we fear what we imagine will happen to us while using it. I refer to this as "phonaphobia."

Dr. Susan Jeffers has written an interesting book on the subject of fear, entitled *Feel the Fear And Do It Anyway*. Two parts of her work are very helpful in dealing with fear. First, she says ". . . over 90 percent of what we worry about never really happens." In other words, the very things that we worry about most have *less than one chance in ten of becoming a reality*! Second, Dr. Jeffers' work led her to compile the following truths about fear:

A) As I continue to grow, fear of some kind will be part of my life.

B) The only way to get rid of fear of doing something is to go out . . . and do it.

C) The only way I can expect to feel better about myself is to go out and do it.

D) I am going to experience fear whenever I'm on unfamiliar territory, but so is everyone else.

E) Overcoming fear is less frightening to me than the prospect of living with the underlying fear that arises from a feeling of helplessness.

In summary, there are many reasons people tend to

freeze at the mere thought of conducting a telephone conversation with a perfect stranger about their career interests. However, in my experience, there are two concerns that stand out as causing the greatest apprehension:

1. *The fear of not knowing what to say:* "How will I get the conversation started? I just know that the moment I hear my contact's voice, I will freeze or go blank!"

2. *The fear of being asked a tough question or one that can't be answered:* "I can just hear it now. I was just laid off and my contact says to me, 'So why were *you* selected while others got to keep their jobs?'" Or, "I was fired two weeks ago; the contact will ask, 'Why are you out of work?'"

To be sure, these apprehensions are perfectly normal, but do you remember the two people I wrote about in the introduction to this book? (If you haven't read the introduction, I strongly suggest that you do so now.) One person thought that the game was over for him. The other was totally petrified from even thinking about using the telephone to discuss her career pursuits.

There is one word that best describes the most effective way to get rid of these fears. No magic or special talent is required and virtually everyone can do it. However, it's a word so simple that you may be disappointed when you read it. It's *planning*. That's right, planning. Although this word may seem obvious, you can truly rely on it!

Planning will tell you what to say. It will help you anticipate what may go wrong. If done well, planning will make your apprehensiveness go away. I will show you how to do it.

The question is, what does the planning involve? Well, actually not much. Once you have a plan, it will carry you through your telephone networking campaign. In fact, I am sure your fears will disappear, and you will find that the real challenge (and potential pitfall) to be the possibility of coming across as *too polished*! That's right. You can actually master telephone networking skills so well that you may sound too good, like a professional interviewee.

Let me show you what I mean. After a couple of weeks, my seminar participants are invited back to discuss their successes and failures. I remember one participant in particular who made the following statement: "I've found that the problem is not so much about being afraid of what will happen. I am now concerned with sounding like a radio talk show host. How do I deal with this?" (You will find the answer to this question in the chapter entitled, "Pitfalls.") So you see, the challenge is not overcoming your fears. The *real* challenge is to remain *conversational* with *every* contact and to project both confidence and sincerity.

A nice problem to have, right? You will have this problem too, if you develop a plan.

There is one other important point about our reluctance to use the telephone. We forget about the key message communicated every time we pick up the telephone to expand our network. This message, one that you transmit loud and clear, is that you are taking charge of your future. You communicate this before the very first word is spoken, and it speaks louder than anything else you can say about yourself. The message says you are *proactive*. You are not satisfied to sit around and *let* things happen. Rather, you are determined to *make* them happen. When the decision comes down to you and someone else who appears to have equal ability and experience, you can bet your actions will result in you being favored when the final votes are cast.

Let's look next, in Chapter 2, at the significance of this message within the overall hiring process.

CHAPTER 2

WHAT IT ULTIMATELY BOILS DOWN TO: CHEMISTRY

Like it or not, you are in the process of marketing the finest product or service you know of: yourself. Regardless of the circumstances surrounding your career search, keep in mind that you are marketing a quality product or service. And somewhere, not so far away, someone has a need for your product. So what are you waiting for? Let's start the telemarketing process.

I prefer to think of what you are doing as *marketing* and not selling, since there is very little actual face-to-face encounter with the hiring executive. Don't get me wrong. Your ultimate goal is *landing* a position or specialty that is right for you, and this is analogous to closing a sale. However, marketing covers all the factors that make a product or service remain in the minds of the buying market. Much of this is done before actually introducing the product to the market place. That's what you have to do. Through telephone networking, you can create a market presence to make your buying market aware of both your availability and capability. The larger the network, the greater the presence, and the quicker you will find what you are looking for. (Again, it's good to keep in mind that what most people are so skittish about is asking directly for a job over the phone. As you can see, the focus of this campaign is on *building positive awareness of you candidacy* within target companies.)

Of course, one can create market presence via broadcast mailings of resumes and cover letters. Unfortunately, the return on time invested is minimal at best. Here is what William J. Morin, Chairman of Drake, Beam, Morin (a large outplacement firm with headquarters in New York City) was quoted as saying in his article, "How to Use the Telephone to Find and Get the Job You Want," which appeared in the *National Business Employment Weekly*.

> "In a standard broadcast letter mailing, only an average of about 50 percent to 60 percent of letters get read by the proper person . . . . From tracking follow-ups, our studies show that some 20 percent of the letters are lost in transit, sidetracked by secretaries, or left in the mailroom. About another 30 percent to 40 percent go to the wrong person who may not take the time to reroute them."

He concluded the article by saying, "It [using the telephone] not only helps speed up the job search, but it is the fastest way to get immediate feedback on what you are doing. You will also discover what jobs are available, because you will be tapping the 'hidden job market,' allowing you to pre-sell yourself for unadvertised jobs."

In telephone networking, unlike broadcast mailings, you are doing some significant things that separate you from the rest of the fine people represented in that pile of resumes on your future employer's desk:

1. *You are demonstrating initiative.* This sends a very clear message to your contact that you are a self-starter. You know what you want and are not content to wait and let corporate culture take its course.

2. Through personal telephone contact, *you become a*

living, breathing human being, who can speak the language, establish rapport, and perhaps even demonstrate a sense of humor. In short, it is all of those things that make you a real, live person.

3. *You are beginning to build "personal chemistry,"* which is an important part of the overall hiring process. This is especially true when you are being compared to a *job specification,* which is a document that describes the knowledge, skills, education, and work experience that one must have to fill a specific position. It is a description of the "perfect person" for that position, *and we all know that person does not exist*! That being the case, the question now becomes, "What trade-offs is the hiring executive willing to make?" First, he knows the perfect person for the position doesn't exist. Second, there is a person sitting across the desk who *very nearly* fits the specification, while at the same time projecting a positive self-image. In other words, the employer would be inclined to say, "This is someone I can work with."

In summary, the name of the game is marketing. We want to make your market aware of your availability as soon as possible. The fastest way to make that happen is to use the telephone.

Next, let's see what a tailor-made telephone networking plan looks like!

CHAPTER 3

THE PROCESS

We are going to get you to a point where networking telephone calls becomes as natural to your daily routine as breathing. But to do this, you need a process. "Winging it" is not the way to accomplish this. As a matter of fact, I would be willing to bet that much of the fear and apprehension felt when considering whether to spontaneously call someone arises because we can't imagine what we would say to that person. Why? Because we haven't given it any forethought. In other words, we see ourselves winging it . . . and . . . we don't see ourselves as being very good at it. However, *telephone networking is a skill,* one you can learn. With a step-by-step process, you can become very effective at it in less time than you can imagine.

Here are the basic steps in the telephone networking process:

1. *Knowing your objectives:* This includes the position you are seeking, and two specific goals you want to accomplish during the meeting.

2. *Knowing who to call:* This section describes the people who can offer you the most help and how to find them.

3. *Knowing what to say:* Here, you learn how to get the

conversation started so that you do not come across as begging for a job.

4. *Dealing with the challenges:* This process includes anticipating how you will handle such innocent questions as, "Is this about a job?," "What company shall I say you are with?," "Why are you out of work?," or "What sort of salary are you looking for?" The key to fielding these questions is *anticipation!*

5. *Getting a commitment:* As one author says, "You don't want to look good on paper; you want to be good in person." Your objective is to get a face-to-face meeting with your contact. You want him or her to meet you as a person and not just look at your resume. A commitment to meet with you is a logical and natural conclusion to the process outlined above. All you have to do is make an appointment.

6. *Improving:* Regardless of the outcome of each call, the process must include a step that asks, "If I could make the call over again, what would I say differently?" *This final step will reduce the time required to find the right position for you than any other in the process.*

The remainder of this book will cover each step of the process in detail. This will provide you with the necessary tools to speak to those who know the people who can get you back to work. So let's get started.

CHAPTER 4

WHO DO I CALL? WHERE DO I GET MY CONTACTS?

The number of potential contacts you have to work with is enormous. You don't really need very many to get started. *By making a commitment to get at least two names from each person you talk to,* you will have all the names and contacts you can handle! As a matter of fact, networking begins with a surprisingly small nucleus of contacts. The question is, Who are these contacts and where can you find them?

There are a number of potential sources available to you. These include:

- ❑ family
- ❑ friends
- ❑ neighbors
- ❑ fellow church members
- ❑ members of your civic club/fraternal organization
- ❑ hair stylist/barber
- ❑ past/present business associates
- ❑ alumni associations
- ❑ fellow members of professional associations and societies

- ❑ fellow hobbyists
- ❑ people you meet while traveling
- ❑ people in the news who have recently been promoted within you industry
- ❑ hiring decision makers in related specialties who are running recruiting ads

Your local library also has a wealth of references upon which to draw. These include as follows:

1. The *Dun and Bradstreet Publication Volumes I, II & III* — Generally speaking, these volumes are arranged according to business size. The section containing the green pages is an index for all three volumes. Thousands of companies are listed in alphabetical order according to company name. The individual company listings contain the necessary information to contact them. This necessary information includes *names of key executives*, sales volume, employee population, and type of business. Since this material is constantly updated, it would be wise to check with the company's receptionist regarding the accuracy of names and positions contained within the references.

2. The *Dun & Bradstreet Reference Book of Corporate Managements* — This is an excellent biographical reference on *specific members* of top management within the above mentioned companies. This reference will supply you with such personal data as educational background, club affiliations, as well as any political activities and related involvements. The people being profiled are presidents, chief executive officers, vice presidents, and other members of top management. These names are extremely important to you when contacting a company for the first time, as I will show in Chapter 11.

How might you go about using one or more of these references?

First, determine *where* in the country and in what field of endeavor you want to work. This will help to focus your search. Next, determine the size of the company you want to work for. Then, use one of the references mentioned above. You might also consult a state industrial guide, such as the *Massachusetts Directory of Manufacturers* published by Commerce Register, Inc. of Midland Park, New Jersey. Companies are listed alphabetically by town. This directory will provide the company name, address, telephone number, products, sales, and perhaps the names of a few key members of management.

Generally speaking, I started with the companies closest to me, listed by town in the state industrial guides. By doing so, if an opportunity arose, it would more likely be close to home.

Record the information and create a list of the companies you intend to contact for the next week, month or whatever time frame is comfortable. However, this is your opportunity, so select what you want and go after it.

It's important to keep in mind that many available positions have not been posted on company bulletin boards or appeared in the classified ads. These are "positions-in-the-making," and in many cases, the *employees* of the company do not know these positions exist. This is not because the information is being withheld. In many cases, it is because the position has been approved but is, as yet, unpublished. This is known as the "hidden job market." The hidden job market may also include positions available to the internal organization. These positions are, as yet, unfilled, because no one within the organization has the required skills, education, experience, or background.

The hidden job market is estimated to represent approximately 80 percent of the opportunities that are actually available to the career seeker. The classified ads are not even a vague approximation of the opportunities available to you. There is much, much, more out there waiting for you. Let's say 80 percent of the available job market is hidden. The more companies you identify, the more opportunities you will uncover. Don't think you've completed things if you rush out to get a copy of your local newspaper for the classified ads, since this only represents a fraction of the real opportunities available to you. The personal contacts listed above, as well as your local library, can be very helpful to you in uncovering that market.

Jeff Mead, a good friend and perhaps one of the finest career counselors I have ever met, once told me, "Howard, there are plenty of strings out there. You just haven't pulled them yet!" I found that he was absolutely right. So let's get busy and start pulling those strings!

PLAN OF ACTION

The following is a brief summary of the steps you must take for effective telephone networking:

1. Decide where you want to work.

2. Try to get a firm handle on the size of the company you want to work for. (Taking these first two steps will help a lot in focusing your efforts instead of taking a shotgun approach to getting another job.)

3. Make a list of family, friends, business associates, etc. that you feel comfortable calling. Set a target of no less than five and no more than ten contacts per day. If you contact more than ten, your follow-up work will become so burdensome that you will inevitably get behind and become burnt-out and discouraged.

4. Visit your local library and ask to see the reference section containing business and industrial guides. You might also tell the librarians what you are

doing and ask for their suggestions to help you get started in the right direction. (For example, "I am researching career opportunities in sales and marketing and would like to see some industrial guides or business directories that will provide names addresses and phone numbers of specific companies within the Boston area.")

5. Call the people you know first. As a matter of fact, make a point of *always* calling the easiest contact first! By doing so, you have taken the path of least resistance in starting the day's calling. You have now established momentum, and the second call will be much easier to make.

CHAPTER 5

FOCUS! FOCUS! FOCUS!

Before you begin to establish a telephone network, it is extremely important for you to set an objective in terms of the kind of work, position, specialty, profession, or career field you want to embark upon. The reason for this is simple. You attempt to contact people with the express purpose of meeting with them, so that they can direct you to the people who can offer positions to you. To impress these contacts, you have to sound *driven* in the direction of the position. The unspoken message you are communicating is that you know what you want, and you are determined to get it without waiting around for it to beat your door down.

Imagine for a moment that you are a hiring executive by the name of Mr. Jones, and you receive a telephone call that goes something like this: "Good morning, Mr. Jones! My name is Howard Armstrong, and the reason for calling you is that I am conducting research on career opportunities in the area of . . . well . . . to tell the truth . . . my experience is pretty broad . . . but I am interested in pursuing opportunities in sales and marketing. Actually I have had extensive experience in both sales and sales management. Come to think of it, I have also done considerable work in sales and sales management training. I have also worked as a product manager and marketing manager. So, I guess what I am saying is that if you know of any opportunities in any of these areas, I would appreciate your giving me a couple of minutes of your time to sit down with me to discuss any of these that may exist. If not, perhaps you can provide me with a couple of names of people I can call in the event they are aware of any opportunities that may exist."

Now, if *you* received that call, what would your impression of the caller be? *My* gut feeling would be that this person is on a fishing expedition and will take anything he or she can get. And that sounds like desperation to me. Now, you may be shaking your head saying, "But, in a way, that's true! I need to find a position as quickly as possible. I'm afraid that if I don't mention all of my skills, positions held, and experience, I may very well lose an opportunity."

Though I agree that it is important that you operate from a position of strength (that is, exploit every opportunity within your capability), the point I am making is that the telephone is no place for a data pump. Remember, your *call objective* is to get a face-to-face meeting with the contact. Have a specific position in mind and call with the intent of getting a face-to-face meeting with your contact based on that. Once you are in the meeting, *then* you can tell him or her about your experiences.

You are probably beginning now to understand the importance of getting the face-to-face meeting in the first place. Not only are you building personal chemistry, but a personal resume that goes far beyond what any paper resume can do. In your face-to-face meeting, you can respond to specific questions, laugh at your contact's humorous statements, ask questions, crack jokes, pause before answering questions, and do any number of other things that will contribute to making *you* a real person that any organization would be proud to have, instead of that *other person* (represented in the form of a resume on your contact's desk).

When I advocate being focused, I really mean two things. First, be focused in terms of communicating the pursuit of a *specific occupational endeavor*. Second, be focused in terms of your *call objective*! And that is *not* to get a job offer over the phone, but *to get a face-to-face meeting with your contact*, even if they do not have an opening. That's right! *Even if they do not have an opening!*

Think about it. Are there any benefits to meeting with someone in a position to hire people with your skills but who has no immediate openings? You bet there are!

PRACTICE
The most obvious benefit is that you get practice in meeting and speaking with hiring executives, and practice builds confidence! This experience is invaluable, because when the real opportunity comes along, you will have met several people who have hiring authority. Consequently, you will not be as nervous in speaking with them about the same things you have been talking to other people about.

GET VALUABLE INFORMATION
Another benefit is that you can get some valuable information from these people. For example, you can find out what they think a successful candidate "looks like" as well as what kind of educational background, work experience, attitudes, and so on this person must have. You can find out what they consider to be the criteria for success for a given specialty. You can also ask them why people in your specialty haven't "made it." In other words, this contact can tell what major factors caused others *not* to succeed. Jack Falvey, in the book mentioned in the Introduction, says a good question to ask the contact is, "What would you do if you were in my position?" In other words, "Here is what I am doing. What would you recommend that I do differently?" You can also ask them *how the future looks* for your specific career field. Given the present set of economic conditions, what is the availability of skilled people, market trends etc., and where does your contact see it all going?

POSSIBILITY OF AN ALTERNATIVE POSITION

A personal experience of mine in this area will illustrate this point.

As an independent contract trainer, I spend much time on the telephone selling my services. During one of my prospecting campaigns, I called the local office of Drake Beam Morin, Inc., one of the largest outplacement firms in the U.S. The company provides outplacement services for companies that have undergone major reorganizations, downsizings, or reductions in force. Their services are designed to provide support and assistance for the separated employees by helping them in many ways, ranging from assistance in resume writing to providing seminars on "Picking the Right Company," "Personal Finance," "Networking Strategies," and so on. So naturally, when I heard that they conduct seminars for their clients, I wanted to see if I could provide training services.

My first contact was the Vice President of Operations for the local office. My strategy here was identical to that which I have been presenting, namely . . . *get in to speak with her face-to-face.* I was determined to meet with her *even if she did not have an opportunity for me.* She agreed to schedule a meeting with me.

The meeting went well. We talked for about an hour and a half, discussing my background, DBM's market and services, and other issues. She told me that they were in the process of selecting additional consultants. This was due to a recent increase in work load as a result of several high-tech reorganizations. She also said that she would get back to me regarding her decision to use my services. A few weeks later, she called to tell me that DBM did not intend to use my services. I did not have career counseling or outplacement experience, and the other individuals she met did have this experience. But she went on to say, "However, this does not mean that we won't change our minds three months later, if we decide that your background fits our needs." Right! I've heard that one before, too!

The next day I made it my number one priority to send her a thank-you note expressing my appreciation for the opportunity of meeting with her. In this note, I also mentioned that I would follow up on the referrals she had given me. The note had barely had time to hit her desk when I received a call from her asking, "Have you ever done any work in telemarketing?"

By now you have probably guessed the outcome. I wound up conducting several telephone networking seminars for DBM. There are three very important reasons why I believe that happened. First, I insisted on meeting her face-to-face. Second, during our meeting, I somehow managed to convince here that I was a human being who looked and sounded very much like the human beings conducting their career counseling seminars. Third, I had telemarketing sales background. Put it all together, and you have an answer to a problem that her office was experiencing: namely, her clients needed someone with sales and telemarketing experience to motivate them to use the telephone to spearhead their networking attack. Mind you, I called with the specific request of meeting with her to discuss career counseling seminars. Her conclusion was to combine my skills and experience to *create a new kind of seminar for her clients*!

I guarantee you that I would not have been hired if I had not pressed for a meeting. Despite the fact that I did not fill the minimum requirements of experience as a career counselor/consultant, *I did make an impression, which resulted in my being offered an alternative position*. This position was *created* for the express purpose of using my experience to solve a specific problem they were experiencing.

REFERRALS

Make it a habit not to leave your contact's office until you have requested the names of two more people to contact, because *this is your third objective*! An effective network cannot survive without the names of people to call. Make it your personal challenge to build that network by getting no less than two names from every person you network with. If you do that, I can assure you you will be successful in your efforts and will greatly reduce the time required to find the right opportunity.

LOOKING GOOD IN PERSON—NOT ON PAPER

By building personal chemistry, you will begin to set the wheels in motion in your contact's mind. And who knows where that may lead? At best, the contact could become so impressed with you that he literally creates a position, because he is not about to let this opportunity (you!) slip through his fingers. At the very least, it could mean a couple of names of people with whom he would like to see a valuable person like yourself working.

The bottom line of meeting with someone who doesn't have a position to offer is that you are getting some valuable practice while at the same time presenting yourself as a living, breathing human being with skills, experience, training, value systems, and a lot of intangibles that can only be defined as personal chemistry.

In summary, you must be focused. You must have a clear idea of the position you want to communicate over the telephone. If you have multiple skills, let them come out during the meeting (not over the telephone).

Focus on your call objective *before* making the call. In every case, your objective should be to get a face-to-face meeting with your contact, even if he does not have an opportunity available. In fact, I would venture a guess that your chances of contacting someone who does have an opening (in your specific area of expertise) on the particular day you call is about one in a million! *And that's good, because once he is aware that you know that no positions are available, any potential barriers of resistance come tumbling down. This is because your contact knows you won't be pressuring him or her for an opening.*

However, the chances of this contact knowing someone who *does* have an opportunity that is just right for you is far greater. And, with names in hand, you will have a referral to make the introduction to that meeting that much easier.

Which leads me once again to your third area of focus, your referrals. It bears repeating: Don't leave without them! Your referrals are what will uncover a major part of that hidden job market we spoke of in the introduction to this book.

PLAN OF ACTION

Before making the first call, decide what kind of work you are pursuing. Remember that the specific position's being not available is irrelevant. It's the meeting and the contacts you want, and the chance to leave a positive impression in the minds of these contacts.

CHAPTER 6

SCRIPTING

Now that you have some idea of how to locate your contacts and what your objective will be in calling them, the question becomes, "What do you say?" As a matter of fact, this is the area my seminar participants claim is one of the most difficult for them: getting the conversation started.

You feel awkward, but you don't want to sound awkward. There is the element of stage fright you feel in the pit of your stomach. You just want to meet people face-to-face and expand your network. Yet somehow speaking those words over the telephone seems like "mission impossible."

This is where a script comes in handy. Now, when I say "script," I don't mean the kind we have all been exposed to at home on a Sunday evening (someone calls from XYZ Publishing Co. to sell magazine subscriptions). Just listening to the caller's voice gives you the impression that you are number 99 in a list of 100 people to be called for that day. Instead of being spoken to, you feel as if you are being processed. That's not what I have in mind when I refer to scripting.

By scripting, I mean having something in writing that

is readily available when you need it. This can be a word-for-word verbatim statement, notes on a 3 x 5 index card, or some sort of checklist. It is important to *have something in writing to refer to*!

I remember very clearly an incident during a one-on-one coaching session following one of my seminars. One of the seminar participants came into my office and said he would like to make an actual call while I was there, so that I could critique his call first hand. I said, "Fine. However, before you make your call, let me ask you a couple of questions."

"First of all, what is your objective in making this call?" He said, rather proudly, "To get a face-to-face meeting with this guy."

Then I asked, "Do you have a script?" He said, "No, I've got a pretty good idea of what I want to say, so I'm going to do without it." I said, "Fine."

He dialed the number. I could tell that the first person he spoke to was the receptionist, and the second person was his contact's secretary. To this point, he seemed poised and confident. But I knew exactly when the contact came on the line. The caller's speech rate increased, his tone of voice went up, and his word selections were rough and tentative. Worst of all, I knew this was not the way he wanted to be perceived. After a few moments, the caller seemed to relax and become himself.

After the call was over, I again asked him a few questions. "What did he like about the call?" He replied, "The fact that I got a commitment for a meeting." "What didn't he like about the call?" He answered, "Well, I felt a bit uncomfortable at first. I think I came across a bit ragged." "If you could make the call again, what would you do differently?" He replied, "I would have a script in front of me, because the words were not there when I needed them."

There is something unique about the reality of hearing the contact's voice at the other end of the telephone. When you're unprepared, it can hit you like a ton of bricks. You *know* you are going to talk to this person. You have known about it for days. You know your objective. However, for some reason, something strange happens when you actually hear that person's speaking voice. And that something strange is why you need a script.

At this point you may be thinking, "So what's the big deal? He got the meeting, didn't he?" Of course, the answer is "Yes." However, he expressed that he was uncomfortable in struggling to find the words he needed to express himself clearly and confidently. It's this discomfort I am concerned about, since it relates to *tomorrow's* activities.

Let me show you what I mean. I'm a jogger. I love to run about three miles a day, because that's a comfortable distance for me to run and still enjoy it. Because I enjoy it, I'm motivated to do it again and again. But let's say that on this particular day I over-extend myself by running five miles. I feel the strain and worse, the next day I feel the stiff muscles. How am I going to feel about running tomorrow? Probably not as enthusiastic because of those stiff, sore, aching muscles. They are very vivid reminders of *how uncomfortable this activity can be*! Now, here's the connection. When it comes time to *begin* the networking process tomorrow, you will remember the discomfort you experienced in making that first call today. The result? Procrastination. "Ah, the heck with it. I'll start again tomorrow and get a fresh start."

The script is valuable, and not just in helping you comfortably begin the conversation today. The script will also serve as a pleasant reminder tomorrow when you start thinking about making your calls and ask yourself, "Now, how am I going to get the conversation started? No problem . . . I've got a script!" The result is that the fear of not knowing what to say will disappear instead of discouraging you from making those calls!

Again, the script does not have to be a word-for-word statement of what you will say. It can take any form you want it to. However, it should be nearby and in a format that is easy for you to use.

My personal preference is to use a word-for-word statement. After I have written it, I usually spend a few minutes reading it to myself out loud. Sometimes I'll write something that looks good on paper, but sounds awful when I say it. So I'll change it. Then I'll say it out loud until I am comfortable with it. Once I feel comfortable with the written statements, I know I'm ready to make those telephone calls.

It's important to keep in mind that by taking the time to write out a script, you are eliminating one of the major elements of "phonaphobia," which is really a kind of stage fright. We envision ourselves on stage without a script. In our mind, we see ourselves picking up the telephone and calling someone in a managerial position. This person has hiring authority, and we see ourselves stumbling over our words in trying to sound intelligent to this all-important person. However, we have no difficulty writing this person an "intelligent letter" in full confidence that we are saying exactly what we want to say. The challenge I put before you is: Why can't you do that with a script? The truth is, *you can!*

Remember the woman who asked for referrals, only to hear the contact say, "Not until I have had a chance to meet with you myself first"? He was so impressed with how well she handled herself that he wasn't about to let this opportunity get away. She simply took the time to write out on paper, in her own words, a message she felt comfortable delivering. Then she made the call. Simple as that. The key to *her* confidence was that she prepared and rehearsed before making the call. How much preparation and revision goes into those letters you write? Why not invest half the time in a script and get far better results in a fraction of the time? Believe me, you can do it!

Keep in mind what I said in the introduction. A well thought-out script is an extremely powerful tool in telephone networking. This is true, since it offers a solution for what intimidates us most about calling someone important. A script lets you know what to say to get the conversation going. Once we've done that, the rest is easy. The toughest part is over. When you are relaxed, you can concentrate on asking whatever questions you want and actually listen to what the contact says in response to those questions.

The truth is, once you have tried this approach, you will be sold not only on its effectiveness but also on its simplicity. Now a word of caution. Remember, I also said that there is a pitfall associated with scripting and telephone networking. That is the danger of becoming too relaxed and smooth. When you sense this is happening to you, the first order of business is to slow down. The last impression you want to give is that you are so comfortable with the process that you sound like you've been doing this for years. Believe me, that's not the way you want to sound!

At this point, I would rather not get into the nuts and bolts of what you *should* say. I will address this in another chapter. I do want to suggest (strongly) that you follow two very simple guidelines when putting your script together:

1. Be yourself.

2. Tell the truth.

That's it. If you try to embellish the facts or sound like someone else, your contact will see right through it. On the other hand, when you say something that sounds natural (and therefore, comfortable for you), confidence and conviction will be the messages your contact hears the loudest.

Here's something else to consider. So far, I have limited the discussion to scripting for *outgoing calls*. Seminar participants often ask, "What about incoming calls?" For example, suppose you have placed a call to a contact you've never spoken to before, and the person was out of the office. You leave word for them to return your call. You can't just say, "My reason for calling you is . . . ," because obviously they're calling you. Should you prepare a script for them as well?

My answer to both questions is "yes." I use a modern miracle of technology called post-it notes, which I stick strategically on the shelf over my telephone. If I call some-one who happens to be out, I simply write the person's name on the note together with my scripted introductory statement. Then, when he or she returns my call, I can simply refer to the note that corresponds with the call I made to him.

Don't let the fact that the contact is initiating the call throw you. For all intents and purposes, the wording of the script is basically the same. The difference is that your wording at the beginning of the call will change a little, be-cause he is calling you. For example, when Mr. Jones returns your call, you would say something like, "Yes, good morning, Mr. Jones, and thank you for returning my call. My reason for having called you earlier is . . ." (and refer to your script for your introductory statement). It's just that simple, as long as you plan ahead for this possible situation. As a matter of fact, I believe one of the conclusions you will come to regarding fear of the telephone is that it really boils down to anticipation. The same holds true regarding some of the other challenges you will be faced with from time to time. (We will be covering those topics in more detail in Chapter 8.)

PLAN OF ACTION

Here's one possible opening statement.

"Good morning, Mrs. Anderson. My name is Howard Armstrong. My reason for calling is that in a couple of weeks I will be throwing my hat in the ring as a candidate for a position in marketing management. Last week, I was speaking to a mutual friend of ours, John Blake, who said that you might be able to spend a few minutes with me on the phone to help me to prepare myself for a career search. Do you have a couple of minutes?"

Now obviously, those are not your words. Therefore, if

you read them out loud they would probably come out sounding hollow and dead. Why? Because they're not your words or expressed in your personality. They're just not you! If you were to say essentially the same thing, how would you say it?

Review the introductory statement above out loud two or three times. Then ask yourself, "How would I say the same thing using my own words?" Next, rewrite the statement and say it out loud again. How does it sound? If it's uncomfortable, try it another way. Keep revising until it sounds like you and feels comfortable.

In the next chapter, I will provide more suggestions for opening statements. For now, this exercise will demonstrate how you can express what you want to say comfortably when beginning a networking telephone call to someone with whom you have never spoken with before.

CHAPTER 7

GETTING THE CONVERSATION STARTED

How do you begin? What do you say?
The information contained in this chapter and Chapter 8 ("Handling Tough Questions and Challenges") will probably do more to help reduce your fear about picking up the telephone and calling someone you have never met or spoken to before than anything else in this book.

For most people, the two toughest parts of the call are getting the conversation started and dealing with the tough questions that you know you will be asked.

This chapter deals with the first concern. I provide some guidelines on how to get the conversation started so that you will feel much more comfortable about picking up the telephone and calling someone you do not know.

First, keep in mind that you are now *researching* what and who is out there. By speaking to as many people as you can, you find out where the opportunities are and the people who are connected with them. So, let's just say that you are in the "Research Mode" or "Phase I" or whatever classification you want to give it of your career search, because, in essence, *that is the basic philosophy behind the introductory remarks to your contact.*

Another point to remember is that you are not (I repeat, *not*) asking for a job! Your objective is to ask for a face-to-face meeting with someone who either has the authority to make a hiring decision or can refer you to a person who may have that power. Now, you may think that I have a hidden agenda: "Well, I'll *tell* them they're not asking for work, but the truth is I just want them to make a lot of calls, because sooner or later they will contact someone who has a job for them." If you think this, you are in for a very big disappointment!

The value of telephone networking is its ability to present you to as many people as possible in the shortest possible period of time. These people, in turn, can refer you to the people who can offer you the right career opportunity or position. *The people that your contacts refer you to* represent that "hidden job market" we talked about in an earlier chapter. These are the people who are about to put a notice on the bulletin board announcing a position that just opened. There could also be a position about to be created that is just right for your skills, and your contact may know the people who are about to put the wheels in motion.

Another extremely important point to keep in mind is the use of the information contained in the chapter on scripting. I assume that you will select your most comfortable introductory statement, regardless of whether it is in note form or a verbatim statement. The important point here is to have a good introductory statement.

With these thoughts in mind, how do you begin the conversation?

There is no single answer to this question. I am going to offer a cross-section of sample introductory statements that will, I hope, spark ideas in your own mind concerning how you wish to phrase your statement. Sometimes changing a word or two is all that is needed to generate a simple introductory statement, one that will get the conversation going. You will notice that in the first few examples of statements I have underlined certain words. These words are key to the basic meaning of the statement itself and may serve as key words for use in your note-form script.

SAMPLES OF INTRODUCTORY STATEMENTS THAT ARE APPROPRIATE WHEN BEING REFERRED BY SOMEONE ELSE

"Good morning, Mr. Jones! My name is Howard Armstrong and I am calling on the *recommendation of* (referral's name). She told me that *no* career *research* effort in the area of (your specialty) *would be complete* without having spoken to you first."

"Good morning, Ms. Smith! You don't know me, but it appears that we both *have* an *acquaintance* in *common* in (your referral). The other day, I was telling him that I was part of the *recent down sizing* at XYZ Company and *to re-enter the job market,* I had to do a considerable amount of *pre-work* and research in the field of (your specialty). He *suggested* that *I get in touch* with you."

"Good morning, Mr. Adams! My name is Howard Armstrong. How are you this morning? Mr. Adams, I am currently *researching career opportunities* in the field of (your specialty) and *through* my *networking activities met* a gentleman by the name of Dave Williams *who mentioned* that *you* may be able to *provide* some *valuable insight* to this *Phase I* career research activity that I am currently engaged in."

"Good morning, Mrs. Simms! The reason for my calling you is that while I was in for a checkup with my physician, Dr. (your referral), she suggested that I call you. You see, I am currently conducting networking activities around the (your specialty) field. When she learned of my area of interest, she *suggested that I give you a call.*"

"Good morning, Mr. Seymour! (Your referral) told me to call you after I told her that I needed to *talk to as many people as possible* concerning the field of (your specialty) to determine if I really want to pursue a career in this area."

"Good morning, Miss Conway! A friend of yours and mine, (your referral), *suggested rather strongly that I give you a call, since you have considerable experience in the area* of (your specialty)."

Though none of these examples is phrased to match your personality, I think you can see where I am going with each of these examples. You probably noticed that each was very similar and yet slightly different in content and emphasis. Let's take a closer look at the similarities.

1. "Good morning!" is punctuated with an exclamation mark. The reason is obvious. You want to demonstrate positive self-expectation and enthusiasm.

2. You always mention your referral (in whatever way is the most comfortable for you) so as to communicate that you both have something in common. This will help to establish rapport very quickly.

3. Refer to your new contact as a valuable potential contributor to your pre-work or research endeavors.

4. State clearly that you are getting information . . . *not asking for a job.* By referring to your activities as "research," "Phase I," or "pre-work," you are in effect bringing the barriers down since you are taking the pressure off the contact to come up with a position for you.

Now let's take a look at some examples of calls that you might make to people you have never met or spoken to before. These are people whose names you may have gotten from any one of the sources outlined in Chapter 4.

These range from newspaper clippings of people who have recently been promoted to individuals named in one of the Dun and Bradstreet or Moody's references.

As an additional tip, be sure to spend a minute with the receptionist to verify that your contact is indeed the person you want to talk to (that is, he or she is still there and in the same position) and *that you have the correct pronunciation of his or her name.* In the event that he or she is no longer in that position due to a recent promotion or transfer to another department, there is no problem. Call the contact anyway and ask who the correct person is to speak to. Only now, *you have a built in referral from someone within the organization!* e.g. "Hello, Ms. Sharp! Ed Smith (your initial contact, and now referral) asked me to give you a call."

Here are some more examples:

> "Good morning, Mr. Jones! My name is Howard Armstrong and, sir, my reason for calling is this: You may be aware of the recent reorganization that occurred at ABC Corporation of which, unfortunately, I was a part. I am presently conducting research on career opportunities in the field of (your specialty) and would like to have the opportunity to meet with you for about twenty minutes to ask you a few questions regarding specific aspects of my search."

> "Good morning, Mr. Smith! I am calling you as part of my initial phase of researching career opportunities in the area of (your specialty) as I feel it would be to my advantage to meet with several people in your position to expand my network, as well as to learn as much as possible about what it is that decision-makers like you are looking for in a successful candidate."

> "Good morning, Ms. Logan! My name is (your name), and I am currently conducting research on career opportunities in the area of (your specialty).

Tell me, would you be the right person to speak to about that?"

"Good morning, Mrs. Blake! My name is (your name). We have never met. However, my reason for calling you is that I am currently in a career transition, and I find myself doing a great deal of pre-work in preparation for a formal search for a position. My pre-work involves speaking to and meeting with several people in your position to discuss such things as your description of a successful candidate in (your specialty), what you might do if you were in my situation, and how you would research the field."

"Good morning, Mr. Hughes! This is (your name) speaking. Mr. Hughes, even though you don't know me, I would like to request your assistance in a matter of importance to me. You see, I have recently left a company in the position of (your previous position), and I am at a crossroads in my career. No, I am emphatically not asking for work. To the contrary, my reason for calling is that I am not even sure at this point whether or not to pursue a career in (your position). You know how things are in our industry. This brings me to why I am speaking to you. You see, I am making a point of speaking to and meeting with several people in your capacity who may be able to shed some light on the future of our industry and positions like mine within it."

"Good morning, Mrs. Hall! My name is (your name), and I see in the paper this morning that XYZ's (her company) stock just jumped up (x points). Your number of employees must be growing! Now let me allay your fears. I am not a salesman. I am not a headhunter. The fact is I am someone who is looking to speak and meet with several people like you who, I believe, can be of assistance. You see, I am at a crossroads in my career, but I am not asking for work. I am asking for about twenty minutes of your time, when it is convenient, to help me get my ducks in a row before I embark on a formal career search. The idea is to have the opportunity to ask you some questions, which will furnish me with some valuable information and better prepare me for the pursuit of a position in (your specialty)."

By now, you have probably noticed that there really isn't a whole lot of difference between these six examples and the referral calls.

In summary, what is the structure of an introductory statement?

First: Begin with an enthusiastic "Good morning!" (afternoon, evening, whatever).

Second: Tell them who you are.

Third: Tell them why you are calling.

Fourth: Be sure to assure them that there is no obligation on their part of find work for you.

Fifth: Appeal to their sense of assistance by using phrases, such as "people in your position", "companies like yours," "I believe you can be of assistance," "people with your experience," or simply, "I need help."

In addition to the guidelines provided, I want to remind you of the two ground rules provided in the previous chapter. These are: Be yourself and tell the truth. Embellishing the facts or simply fabricating something so you will have something to say will catch up with you, and such deception can spell disaster to your networking efforts.

Let me make a suggestion about your speaking style. For some reason, many people feel that a business telephone conversation requires a "business telephone voice" (whatever that is). Simply be yourself. If you aren't, it will be quite obvious to your contact. Just because you are speaking to a hiring decision maker does not mean that you must superstructure your sentences or "sound like a professional or business person." Speak simply, as if speaking to a friend for whom you have a great deal of respect.

In a future chapter, I will provide you with some guidelines on how to project an image of positive self-expectation. However, that does *not* mean that you have to come across as someone other than who you really are! You do need to be sensitive to those things that can create a negative image, however. Through the techniques provided, you can steer clear of any behavior that may turn off your contact.

PLAN OF ACTION

1. Study the examples of introductory statements, and then say each one out loud (into a tape recorder if possible). Next, notice which one comes the closest to what *you* might say.

2. Rewrite one or two of the examples in your own words, and again say them out loud (into a recorder if possible).

3. Refine it, tweak it, modify it until it sounds just like you.

4. If none of the suggestions sound close, go through the examples and find individual words that may be comfortable. You can also develop an entirely different example with the following points in mind:

    a. Demonstrate enthusiasm when greeting your contact.

    b. Be specific about the position you want to discuss.

    c. Assure your contact that you are not pressing

them for a job . . . because you aren't!

d. Convey the fact that a face-to-face discussion of no more than 20 minutes can prove to be very helpful to expand your network and improve your job search strategy.

5. Now that you have what you feel is a comfortable introductory statement in its final form, repeat it out loud until you are absolutely 100 percent comfortable with it. How comfortable? Like putting on an old shoe. Like breathing. That's how comfortable you want to be with it.

PITFALL: Do not, under any circumstances, attempt to memorize the scripted introductory statement! I know of no better way to "clank" or "go blank" than to attempt to memorize your script. Not only will you have the voice of your contact to contend with, but you will be loading on additional pressure as a result of trying to remember exactly what it was that you wanted to say. It doesn't add up to comfort, and it certainly will not be perceived as confidence.

CHAPTER 8

DEALING WITH THE CHALLENGES

"Why are you out of work?"

"What company shall I say you are with?"

"Is this about a job?"

"What sort of salary were you looking for?"

"I really don't think I can be of much help to you."

What do you say to such questions?

Keep in mind that the sole reason for calling your contact is to get a face-to-face meeting with him. Therefore, this chapter's purpose is not to provide interviewing techniques. To the contrary, one of the possible pitfalls in your telephone networking strategy is *allowing yourself to be interviewed over the telephone.*

So why have a chapter on dealing with the challenges? There are two reasons for this. First, I want to put challenges into their proper perspective, because (believe it or not), questions and challenges are actually *expressions of interest*! Second, I want to provide some basic guidelines for dealing with challenges or questions in such a way that you can turn (what appear to be) negatives into positives. You will thereby be increasing your chances of landing a meeting with your contact.

Instead of trying to supply you with a complete list of challenges (which is impossible and of dubious value anyway), I want to show you a cross section of the *kinds* of challenges and questions you might hear. This will establish a foundation upon which to build general guidelines to use in dealing with these situations. Once again, you will be able to apply your own word selection and personality to these situations.

Despite this chapter name ("Dealing With The Challenges"), at times you will be confronted with what are not challenges at all, but are simply surprising moments of discomfort or embarrassment. This is not because the questions are sensitive or difficult. Instead, these questions are uncomfortable or embarrassing, *because the caller failed to anticipate them in the first place!*

For example, let's assume that you are out of work and making your very first telephone networking call. Your contact's secretary answers the telephone, and you begin by saying,

> "Hello, my name is Howard Armstrong. May I please speak with Mr. Jones?"

The secretary responds,

> "Yes, you certainly may, Mr. Armstrong . . . and what company shall I say you are with?"

This simple little question can have a paralyzing effect, if you are not prepared for it. And then your attitude becomes, "Oops! What do I say now?"

This chapter is important because I believe that by anticipating the kinds of questions and challenges that you may encounter, you will greatly reduce most of the worries, fears, and apprehensions associated with telephone networking. Anticipating the challenges ahead of time will allow you to think clearly about your answers without feeling the pressure of someone waiting on the other end of the line for your answer.

According to many of my seminar participants, a real concern is the apprehension associated with wondering how to handle *any* question. Therefore, the key to success on this issue is to anticipate as many kinds of questions as you think you may be asked, then think carefully about how you would answer each question. At the same time, you must focus on being yourself and telling the truth.

Here's another side to challenges that you may not immediately notice. Challenges are, in truth, expressions of interest. That's right! Despite the fact that your contact's comment sounds like a negative statement or questions, the truth is that he or she is interested in you.

Perhaps an illustration that is familiar will help. You are home relaxing comfortably in your favorite chair, watching your favorite TV program, and the doorbell rings. As you open the door, a door-to-door salesman greets you. At this point, it really doesn't matter what he is selling . . . you are just not interested! Now, your single most important goal is to get him to LEAVE! You don't dare ask him any questions, because that will only prolong the visit. You certainly don't want to contest anything he says because you know he's trained to handle just about any kind of obstacle you present. So . . . you wait . . . until he has made his pitch, and then you calmly say, "Thanks, but I'm not interested." Of course, some will persist, but the message is still the same: "not interested!"

Now let's take this example a little further. Suppose that while the salesman was talking, you became mildly interested. You don't want him to know that, so you phrase your questions negatively. For example, you might say, "Well that sounds good, but I'm afraid I couldn't afford anything like that." (You don't know what the price is but you are interested in finding out.) Or, you might say, "Yeah, but I bet it *can't* do _____ !" (What you are actually thinking is, "I wonder if it *can* do _____ ?") On the surface, it sounds like you are objecting. However, the truth is that *you . . . are . . . interested!* The same holds true when speaking to someone who throws you (what sounds like) a curve on the telephone. If the contact wasn't interested in you, he would tell you so and end the conversation right away. The contact may also take the easy way out and have the secretary/receptionist tell you that he is not interested in speaking with you at all. In which case, you say, "Thank you," hang up, and call someone else.

Challenges are expressions of interest. Believe it! I only use the word *challenge*, because this is how *the uninformed and unprepared* perceive them! So the order of business now becomes, "How can I make appropriate responses to these 'challenges' in win-win fashion?" To answer that question, let me give you some overall guidelines in dealing with these networking situations, and then we will move on to cover some specific instances. These guidelines are as follows:

1. *Relax!* Remember, they are truly interested in you. Maybe for them . . . maybe for someone else. You simply have to provide them with some information that will satisfy their curiosity about some aspect of you.

2. *Stop and think.* Don't be in a hurry to have an answer just for the sake of having an answer. And by the way, since you are in the research phase of your career search, it is perfectly okay to say, "Gee, I really don't have an answer for that question. Up to now, I really hadn't thought about it."

3. *Be positive.* Your answer should not reflect any negative emotions or sentiment, especially toward your previous employer. You may well have been through a tough time, but your contact is listening very carefully to your word selection. A red flag goes up for hiring decision-makers when your

answer reflects a higher motivation to get out of something than to get into something better. There's a difference! For example, let's suppose your contact asked you why you want to make a change. You could answer, "Well, the place where I had worked before was the pits. There was no room for growth and two-way communication was non-existent." You can make a more positive impression by saying something like, "I am contacting companies like yours because I believe they represent real growth opportunities for a person with my skills." Then be prepared to provide examples of exactly what you mean.

4. *Tell the truth.* No one is perfect, and your contact knows that. To embellish the facts or fabricate something about yourself is simply asking for trouble. On the other hand, objectively stating the facts concerning the reason for your call will naturally arouse some degree of curiosity in your contact's mind. That curiosity will most likely precipitate out in the form of questions or challenging comments.

5. *Be yourself.* Unless you are a professional actor, attempting to come across as someone other than who you are is pretty easy for any hiring executive to detect.

6. *Learn from the call.* Each time you get off the telephone, ask yourself, "What did I do well?," "What did I do not so well?," and "What can I do to improve?" *This is true regardless of the success or non-success you experienced during the call.* As a matter of fact, my personal belief is that more can be learned from what you did right than by analyzing what you did wrong. (There will be more on this when we discuss what to do when you are down.)

Now that you have some general guidelines, let's look

at some specific challenges my seminar participants have experienced. These will give you an idea of what you might hear. We'll also look at how you might deal with these challenges. However, these guidelines are not intended for putting words in your mouth. There is no formula that says, "If they say X, then you should say Y." Rather, I want to give you an idea of the kinds of responses you might give, while emphasizing that *you* provide the exact word selection in regard to your personality and comfort zone.

Once again, this chapter was not written for improving your interviewing skills. It promotes the idea that a key element of successful telephone networking is *anticipating* the types of questions and comments you may experience. It also suggests some general guidelines in dealing with these in a *win-win* fashion. In so doing, you will be increasing your chances of meeting with your contact.

Though it is impossible to cover all situations, I will attempt to provide a reasonable cross-section of the most common types of situations you may encounter.

Your objective throughout this process is to demonstrate positive self-expectation while, at the same time, inverting negatives into positives. Remember, your contact really is interested.

Let's suppose that you were part of a large-scale reorganization that meant you and several others were terminated. Keep in mind that these kinds of decisions are never easy for any company to make. These are business decisions that reflect the company's need to survive. Unfortunately, no one comes to you first to ask how this change will affect you. Instead, this decision was made without your input and control. The question is, "How do you convey that fact in a positive manner?"

"Why were you terminated?"

Possible
response: "Well, it appears that the company had a pretty tough decision to make. Unfortunately, I have

become a part of that decision along with several other people."

Another possible response: "I guess according to what I read in the newspaper, many companies like ours are going through the same thing these days. Frankly, I never thought it would happen to me. However, I've now accepted it, and I am also determined to make the best of this situation."

Now, let's assume that your contact is still not satisfied. There is still an element of curiosity that asks, "Is this person's termination a reflection on personal performance?" However, the question comes out like this:

"Yeah, but how did they decide who gets to stay and who doesn't?"
The only probable difference between this questioner and someone else is that he or she has the courage to ask, while others do not.

Once again, keep in mind that the decision is one in which you had no input.

Possible response: "Well, you know I wondered about that myself. But it appears that the brunt of the selections came out of those groups with . . .

- low seniority
- older members
- young members
- the people from the East (or West, South, North, etc.)
- the people closest to retirement
- the highest degree of redundancy."

65

As you can see, these groups are just that . . . *groups*. Being a part of a group reduction or downsizing is nothing to be ashamed of. Again, it was someone else's decision, independent of your input. Therefore, your response should never show any indication that you are ashamed. Rather, your answer should reflect that though you were not happy with the decision, you have accepted it and are now prepared to move on.

In the next situation, the individual really cannot lay claims to being part of a decision involving a group. Instead, the situation involves an individual who is pressured by the organization to either resign or face inevitable termination. So, the individual resigns. The question now becomes:

"Why did you resign?"
How does one convey this fact while at the same time project positive self esteem and expectation?

> *Possible*
> *Response:* "From the time I . . .
>
> moved to corporate headquarters . . .
>
> was transferred to my new location . . .
>
> received my last review . . .
>
> transferred to my last department . . .
>
> started working for my new supervisor . . .
>
> started to work for XYZ Corp., . . .
>
> began work on the ABC project . . .
>
> . . . it was pretty obvious that my expectations did not match reality. I honestly believe we did everything we could to negotiate our positions. However, in the final analysis, it was obvious that I would be much better off somewhere else."

Now, let's take a closer look at this response. First, you will notice that the statement communicates that at some point in your past, *you* began to notice that something was not quite right. Then, you describe how you tried to reach some sort of middle ground in win-win fashion via negotiation. Next, you state that after all was said and done, you would be better off somewhere else. In other words, you made the decision after much discussion and careful consideration. Notice what you did not say. You did not say, in effect, "Those bums forced me out!" or "They made it impossible for me to do anything but leave." Instead you communicated the following facts: that *you* knew something was wrong; that *you* attempted to negotiate your position; that *you* decided that the best thing to do was to leave; that *you* have accepted that and are now prepared to move on. You have objectively communicated a statement of fact. There is nothing negative about your word selection.

Now, the above described situations still may not fit your situation. Perhaps your situation was more like what happened to me a few years ago. At the time, I was working for a company in New Jersey; we had been acquired by another company that had headquarters in Pennsylvania. Only three months after having been transferred to the corporate headquarters, I was fired. I was not told the exact reason. (Something about "not fitting the corporate mold," or some such thing). It was a difficult situation. Actually, it was more like a nightmare. I had just purchased and moved into a brand new house. And then . . . Bang!

"Why were you fired?"
What was I going to say to people who wanted to know why I was fired? I had made up my mind that I was going to tell them straight out that I *had* been fired and to deal with the challenges as they occurred. By doing so, I knew that if they began thinking seriously about me, I would not have any "back peddling" or "explaining" to do at some later time.

So my response to the question ("What happened?") was, "Well, as I look back, it was obviously a bad match and, frankly, now I feel as though a great weight has been lifted from my shoulders. I'm glad it's over, and frankly, it feels pretty good to be looking for new opportunities."

I told the truth. In retrospect, I knew it was a bad fit, and, all things considered, I felt better about it. These were statements of fact reflecting not only my awareness of the situation, but also my acceptance of it to such a degree that I welcomed the opportunity to get started on a new career path. Notice that *I did not say anything derogatory about my former employer*! Instead, my emphasis was focused on my positive expectation of what I believed the future had in store for me.

Once again, let's not forget our reason for calling. We want a face-to-face meeting with our contact, and somehow we need to steer the conversation in that direction *after every challenge we encounter*. Therefore, an add-on statement to the response given above would be appropriate. There will be more information on how to do this in the chapter entitled, "Asking For The Meeting."

Another area of concern involves salary-related questions. These questions can take many forms. However, a generic cross section will help in anticipating the nature of such challenges.

We all hesitate to reveal our salary preferences. There are two basic reasons. First, we don't want to say "Well, I'm looking for a salary in the area of $40,000," only to find that the position would have offered a $47,500 salary. By saying $40,000, I just negotiated myself down by $7,500. Second, revealing our salary preference could have the opposite effect. You might say, "Well, my salary at XYZ Corp. was $45,000," only to learn that you have been eliminated from consideration, because that figure was higher than the company was prepared to pay. In this case, you might have been willing to take a cut in salary, because you may have honestly believed that this company represented an opportunity that could pay back dividends in the future.

Therefore, besides following the general guidelines offered in this chapter, remember to leave room for negotiating your position in regard to salary issues.

With this in mind, let's look at some examples of how the subject of salary may surface during the call. One of the most common questions your contact might ask is:

"Tell me, what is your salary history?"

Possible
response: "Well, my view is that salary is one of several issues that I will be considering when opportunities surface. It would suffice to say that my previous salary was competitive with the national average for my specialty. I will be in a better position to discuss salary once I have some idea of the requirements for the position being offered."

"But I need to have some idea of the salary you are seeking."

Possible
response: (If your contact is adamant about this point, then give him or her a *range* broad enough to provide you with some latitude for future negotiations.)

"Well, to be honest, I guess I am looking for something in the range of $40,000 to $50,000."

If the hiring decision maker insists on a specific salary (". . . or else we simply cannot move forward with your request for a meeting"), then you might consider the following:

Possible
response: "My salary while working at XYZ Corp. was $25,000. However, one of my primary objectives is to improve on this."

In summary, the most important point presented in this chapter is that you must take the time to anticipate potential questions and challenges. In so doing, you will feel better prepared, and although you may never be able to anticipate all of the possibilities, the chances of your contact *surprising* you with a difficult-to-answer question will have been greatly diminished.

PLAN OF ACTION

For each of the questions and challenges listed below, write down what are comfortable responses for you to each. Don't say what you think the contact wants to hear. Say what you believe is an accurate and objective statement of the facts in words that reflect your personality. Most important, be positive. Remember, every question is a statement of interest, and every challenge, though it sounds negative, can be answered in a positive manner. Just take the time to think about it. Here are these questions:

"What company shall I say you are with?"

"Is this about a job?"

"Why are you out of work?"

"Hello?"

"I really don't think I can help you right now."

"Why is it that you lost your job while others did not?"

"Why should I meet with you?"

CHAPTER 9

ASKING FOR THE MEETING

Asking for the meeting is like payday! It is the basis for your planning and practice. It is also the natural, logical conclusion to your telephone discussion.

The two questions most often asked by seminar participants regarding this part of the process are as follows:

1. When do I ask for the meeting?

2. How do I ask for the meeting?

The "how" is a matter of personal style and, to some extent, trial and error. With time, you can develop a personalized approach that works for you. With regard to the first question, "when," many situations can occur that are excellent opportunities to ask for a meeting. I will describe four of them to you.

Situation #1:
The first is the simplest and most direct. Generally speaking, it will occur when you have made your introductory statement, which is followed by an acknowledgement or brief comment from your contact.

Examples: "Uh huh."

"I see."

"Okay."

Since he or she has offered no reason for *not* meeting you, *now* is the time to ask. Because the conversation to this point has been very brief, you will be tempted to make "small talk" to fill the void of what you had assumed would be a much longer conversation. That's a mistake! Don't waste the contact's time or yours talking about the weather or anything else . . . just request a meeting.

Situation #2:

The second opportunity is similar to the first. However, instead of simply acknowledging your introductory statement, your contact overtly demonstrates his interest by making a positive statement about you, or perhaps, your approach to your career search. When this happens, ask for a meeting!

Examples: "Well, I certainly admire your proactive approach!"

"Yes. Well it sounds like you have a pretty good handle on things!"

"Well, I have to admit, I *do* like the way you come across on the telephone."

"Well, I have to admit, your approach *is* different, but by the same token it certainly is a positive and assertive approach at that."

Situations #3 and #4:

The third and fourth situation examples that I will provide stem from our discussion in the previous chapter. Your contact is masking *real interest* in the form of a question or direct challenge.

Examples: "Why are you out of work?"

"What sort of salary are you looking for?"

"I really can't afford to bring anyone else on board at this time."

Now, because we have anticipated, planned for, and practiced responding to the various types of challenges that we may have to deal with, we are prepared for this . . . *right*? (Right!)

Good. Then the next part is easy. Because, after we respond to their question or challenge, we simply continue by asking for the meeting.

Before I give you some examples of how to ask for the meeting for each of the above situations, I would first like to share with you some general guidelines in asking for the meeting. These guidelines are as follows:

1. Be positive, not apologetic!

2. Summarize your objectives and points agreed upon.

3. Get a commitment.

Now let's take a look at some of the examples.

Situation #1

Caller: "Good morning, Mr. James! My name is (your name). My reason for calling you is that having been affected by the recent reorganization at XYZ Corp., I am conducting a great deal of pre-work in researching career opportunities in the field of (your specialty). In so doing, I am both speaking to and meeting with several people in positions similar to yours. I hope to learn from people like you what a successful candidate looks like, as well as what you might do, if you were in a similar situation."

Contact: "I see."

Caller: "So now that you have a pretty good idea of what I am trying to do, I was hoping we could meet either Thursday or Friday of next week. Which is best for you?"

Note that the caller did not become flustered by the brief response, but instead went right into the request. Small talk would only cloud the issue. A confident approach to the request, on the other hand, can work effectively.

Situation #2

Caller: "Good morning, Mrs. Wright! My name is (your name). I am calling because I believe you can help me though my present career transition. As you can imagine, a thorough approach to a career change involves a great deal of pre-work planning and execution. The pre-work phase of my plan has me speaking to and meeting face-to-face with people in your position. I want to learn as much as I can about what you look for in a (your specialty), as well as how you perceive the future for specialties and skills such as mine. After all, you know how this industry is."

Contact: "Well, I certainly admire your proactive approach."

Caller: "Thank you very much. And you are absolutely right. I honestly believe that a proactive approach is necessary to get the information I need to execute my plan. A meeting with you would be very helpful in getting this information. Would you be able to meet with me on Monday of next week or is Wednesday better?"

Notice how the caller didn't just accept the positive response, but rather repeated the phrase, "a proactive approach." In sales parlance, this is referred to as a support statement. Any time a customer makes a positive statement about the sales person, company, product or service, the alert professional will reinforce the statement to demonstrate that he was listening. Even more important, repeating the statement serves to create momentum in the direction the caller wants to go, namely a face-to-face meeting.

Situation #3

Caller: "Good morning, Miss Bell! My name is (your name), and I was told by a mutual friend of ours (your referral) that you would be a valuable asset to my career research in the field of (your specialty)."

Contact: "Yes, (your referral) called yesterday to say that you might be calling today. *What sort of salary were you looking for?*"

Caller: "Well, certainly salary is one of several issues that I will be considering to determine which opportunity best meets most or all of my requirements. Suffice to say I am looking for something in the range of $50,000 to $60,000. However, these are precisely the kinds of issues that I was hoping we could discuss in greater detail in your office. I was wondering if you would be able to meet with me, say, Monday of next week—or is Tuesday better for you?"

Notice that the caller was not discouraged or intimidated by the request for salary. The caller also not only left plenty of room for negotiating, but expressed how salary was one of many details that could be discussed in a face-to-face meeting with the contact. In essence, the caller took a potentially negative situation and changed it into a positive request for a meeting.

Situation #4

Caller: "Good morning, Mr. Jameson! My name is (your name). I am calling at the request of (your referral). He told me that you might be able to provide some valuable insight regarding what a hiring executive in your position

> looks for in the area of (your specialty). I assume you are familiar with my situation as (your referral) mentioned that he would call in advance to brief you on the details concerning the reorganization that affected me at ABC, Inc."

Contact: "Yes, he did call. As a matter of fact, I just got off the phone with (your referral) about fifteen minutes ago. Hey look, I'd really like to help you out, but *I really can't afford to bring anyone else on board at this time.*"

Caller: "Mr. Jameson, I can honestly appreciate your position, and it looks like we have a slight miscue here. You see, I know you don't have any openings, and I am not asking for one. My reason for calling you was to arrange a twenty-minute meeting at no obligation to you, so that you would feel free to discuss those considerations you feel are important in selecting a person in the field of (your specialty). I was also hoping that between now and when we do meet, you might be able to refer me to a few people that I could contact to expand my network. I don't have any meetings scheduled for Tuesday or Wednesday of this week. Which is the most convenient day for you?"

Here again, a potentially negative situation was reversed. The contact seemed to feel obligated to find the caller a position. By clearly stating that there was no obligation on the part of the contact, the caller stands a far better chance of getting a face-to-face meeting.

Now, let's suppose for a moment that you are unsuccessful at getting a meeting. How can you not get a commitment and still be a winner? Simple! Make it your personal challenge to get at least two names from everybody you talk to, regardless of the success of your telephone call. You can say just that to your contact. The last situation we'll examine in this chapter involves the conversation after the contact is unable to commit to a meeting at this time.

Situation #5:

> *Caller:* "Well, Miss Ames, I can appreciate your position. Let me just mention one other thing. You know, I have made it my personal challenge to get a minimum of two names from everyone I speak with to continue to expand my network. What two people outside of your company would you suggest I touch base with?"

That's all there is to it. In this situation, getting two referrals is like a base on balls. You may not have gotten a home run, but you have definitely advanced the runner . . . you!

PLAN OF ACTION

Take out a piece of paper and pen (or pencil) and write the words you feel comfortable using to make your request. Remember, don't sound apologetic, just ask objectively for an appointment for your meeting.

Next, tie that request in with a response you have developed to one of the challenges mentioned in the previous chapter's Plan of Action exercise.

Say it out loud a few times to get used to the sound of your own voice requesting a commitment. Now you are ready to try it!

CHAPTER 10

PROJECTING A POSITIVE TELEPHONE IMAGE

I would like to tar and feather the person who authored the phrase, "You only get one chance to make a good first impression." In my book, that statement is real garbage!

In my judgment, the mere fact that you have picked up the telephone and called is a major step forward in creating an image of positive self-expectation. By making that call, you have separated yourself from all of the "paper jungle" job hunters. You are no longer using a cover letter or resume. You are no longer just a name on a piece of paper that requires "processing." To your telephone contact, you have become a living, breathing, speaking, proactive human being. This is what sets you far apart from the rest of the career hopefuls who camp out by their mailboxes waiting for the benevolent nature of corporate culture to help them along.

Now, since the first step that you have taken is an extremely positive one, let me suggest some techniques that will add momentum to what is already a very successful beginning. How do we create this momentum? By projecting an image that is both positive and confident. This is done through the use of three important ingredients: speech rate, voice tone, and word selection. (A caution is placed on the last one, however, because people tend to get uptight about it if they are concerned about their vocabulary).

Let's begin with speech rate. Chances are that you have probably heard nervous people speaking. And, chances are pretty good their speech seemed hurried, as if they couldn't wait to get whatever was making them nervous over with. You have probably experienced the same thing yourself. The question is, "How do we control our speech rate, so that we do not project an image of nervousness, especially when calling someone for the first time?" Easy! Simply match your speech rate to that of your contact. That's all there is to it! By matching your contact's speech rate, you will not sound different to them. The conversation will move along at a rate that is comfortable for your contact.

Our next ingredient in projecting a positive telephone image is tone of voice. Your voice tone should project positive self-expectation. For example, when the secretary puts you through to your contact, you should say, "Mr. Jones . . . ," with an uplifting question mark tone in your voice. (In contrast with, "Oh, hello, Mr. Jones," with a tone that keeps getting lower with each syllable you speak.) Listen to the tone of your voice. Does it project energy and enthusiasm, or does it have a quality about it that sounds like your puppy dog was run over by a Mack truck? The best way to find out how you sound is to get a tape recorder and tape your networking telephone calls. Listen carefully for anything that could communicate lack of enthusiasm on your part. No one will become any more excited about the call than you. So, if *you* aren't excited, it goes without saying that your contact won't be either.

Our third ingredient is word selection. Once again, the key to success is to project an attitude of positive self-expectation. In essence, we have already covered this subject when we discussed scripting. You spend a lot of time thinking about the right way to say exactly what you want in your cover letters. Take the same care in creating a script that says exactly what you want in a way that you want to say it. If someone overheard our conversation when attempting to "wing it", it might sound like, "Well, gee, Mr. Jones, ah, if you don't mind, that is, if it won't be any problem for you, I would kinda like to maybe get together one day next week. That is, of course, if it's all right with you?" If you were the contact, what would you think? My impression of that caller is that this person really did not have a solid idea of what or how he was going to say what he wanted to. Also, I get the impression of an apologetic lifestyle. We make no apologies when we create our own career path. We simply make up our minds, and then go out and do it.

The caller must make every effort to assert in specific and direct terms exactly what it is that he wants. "Mr. Jones, my purpose in speaking with you today is to have the opportunity to meet with you face-to-face to further explore some of the things we've been talking about. I am free Tuesday and Wednesday of next week. Which is best for you?"

ADDITIONAL TECHNIQUES

Here are a few other points to keep in mind when developing a positive telephone image.

Good posture: Sounds ridiculous, doesn't it? The truth is that your posture influences how you sound on the telephone. If you are slumped over in a chair, your voice will reflect that posture. This is not to say that you cannot be relaxed while making networking telephone calls. Quite the contrary! However, if you are slouched in your chair (or perhaps leaning back while resting your feet on your desk), so that your posture influences your tone of voice, this could create a mental picture in your contact's mind of a person who is less than enthusiastic. And if there is one time you want to be enthusiastic . . . it is now!

Stand up: Standing while making your calls tends to put energy into your conversation. You can't get too comfortable, because you are not in that chair. Your voice will project a consistently alert and enthusiastic attitude that is hard to misperceive as anything other than positive.

Smile while you talk: Listen to a radio announcer or your next caller on the telephone, and see if you can tell when that person is smiling. The fact is that you can almost always tell when he or she is smiling, because voice tone and word selection is usually a dead giveaway. If you smile when you talk (believe it or not), your contact can actually "hear you smiling."

Use a mirror: Watch yourself in a mirror when you make those calls. Notice when you are not smiling, and let this be your cue to put that smile on your face. If you notice that you are frowning, try to pay attention to the tone of your voice as well. Chances are that the image you are projecting is right in keeping with your facial expressions. A mirror can be an excellent reminder of what your face is communicating to your contact.

Use a tape recorder: This is probably the best indication of how you are coming across to your contact. Tape the call. Immediately after the call, play the tape back and ask yourself, "What did I do well?", "What did I do not so well?", and "How can I improve?" A tape recorder can be your best friend in improving the image you project over the telephone.

Notice: Everything in this chapter is a direct reflection of attitude. If your attitude is one of positive self-expectation, then your speech rate, voice tone, and word selection will be working in concert to provide an overall image that says, "You're missing out on a big opportunity, if you don't at least spend a few minutes with me face-to-face!"

CHAPTER 11

GETTING TO THE RIGHT PERSON THROUGH "POSITIVE ERROR"

This technique (Positive Error) once got me out of a potentially dangerous situation. Years ago, I was in the Air Force and flying in a troop support mission in Thailand, which is very close to the Cambodian border. Our objective was to find a small landing strip. This was nothing more than a widened-out portion of a road that ran north-south along the Thai-Cambodian border. We had to land and pick up a handful of Thai troops for transport back to Bangkok. All this took place in an area that had no radio communications or navigation aids of any kind.

To locate the airstrip, we had to fly east until we found the north-south road and then land when we saw the airstrip. This presented us with two problems. First, if the road and airstrip were nowhere in sight, which way should we turn to find the airstrip—north or south? If we flew North, we could find ourselves flying for quite some time before realizing that we were going in the wrong direction, thereby wasting precious fuel and time. If we flew South and saw an airstrip, how would we know it was the right one? And if we followed the road too far South, it would eventually take us across the Cambodian border. Here, there was definitely another airstrip, but one that belonged to the enemy.

To eliminate this danger, we used a technique called "positive error." This meant that as we flew in an easterly direction, we actually turned slightly north knowing that our flight path would take us to the North-South road. However, this was *well north* of the airstrip and the Cambodian border. In other words, we *deliberately flew off course in a safe direction*. Once we got to the road, we turned south and followed the road visually until we arrived at the airstrip.

(For you skeptics who are wondering how we knew it was the *right* landing strip, refer to the Appendix to find out.)

The question in your mind now is probably, "What does that have to do with telephone networking?" Well, it is just this. Let's say that you want to call a particular company because you believe it would add value to your networking activities. However, you don't know who the contact is. You can use a positive error to get the name you need. In other words, you can get to your networking contact by deliberately shooting higher (in the corporate pecking order) than you need to. There are two benefits in doing this. First, you will get to the person you need to speak to. Second, you will actually generate a referral from an organization in which you are unknown. There are two basic ways (with all sorts of variations on the same themes) to do this.

If you are calling a company with 300 employees or less, contact the president or chief executive officer. That's right! Positive error . . . go right to the top! Then when the CEO's secretary answers, simply use the introductory statement you developed back in Chapter 7. If you're put through to the CEO, once again, use your introductory statement. Undoubtedly the response will be, "I'm probably not the person you want to talk to. You probably need to speak with John Smith. He's the head of (your specialty department) and can probably be more help to you than I can." You respond, "Thank you very much. Would it be possible for your secretary to transfer me to that extension?" *What you now have is a referral from the chief executive officer to your contact!* It might sound something like this when your contact's secretary answers: "Ah yes, my name is (your name), and I have been referred to Mr. Smith by (the CEO)." From that point on, the chances are pretty good that you will be put through immediately.

Now, let's suppose that the organization you wish to call has more than 300 employees. What then? The reason I used 300 employees as the cutoff is that in a company of this size, the CEO probably knows every department head by name. Once you get over that number, it becomes a real challenge for him to recall the name of the specific person you need to speak with. This is where the receptionist/operator can be very helpful. These people are walking, talking corporate encyclopedias. They have a wealth of knowledge about the company in terms of its organization as well as the names of specific people within it. Unfortunately, their knowledge (in my opinion) is tragically underexploited. We tend to also think of the receptionist and secretary as the enemy. They're not. They can be the best ally you have, if you approach them with respect and appeal to their sense of assistance.

In this scenario, we will once again use "positive error" to locate the person you need to speak to. In this case, you don't want to speak to the Chief Executive Officer. Instead, *you want to speak to your contact's boss!* And the one person who can help you do this is the receptionist/operator. So, when you call the target organization, your introductory statement might go something like this.

> "Yes, good morning! My name is (your name). I am calling companies like (target organization) to research career opportunities in the field of (your specialty), and I was hoping you could provide me with some information. Actually, if it wouldn't be too much trouble, I need the names of four people. And by the way, if this is not a good time, I can tell you their positions and call back later for the information."

At this point the operator will probably either elect to

provide you with the information if the current call load will allow it, or ask you to call back. In either case, you are on your way. The answer will likely be, "Certainly, I would be glad to help you if you don't mind the interruptions. I will probably have to put you on 'hold' at times, so I can take care of my calls. Now, what are the names you need?" You then provide what you believe your contact's position is, his or her secretary, the name of the person that your contact reports to, and that person's secretary. Upon receiving the information say, "Thank you very much. You have been very helpful!" You are home free!

Next, call your contact's boss. When his secretary answers, you respond with,

> "Yes, is this Theresa Bennett? Great, Mrs. Bennett; I'm glad I was able to reach you directly, as I was told you might be able to help me out. You see I am researching career opportunities in the field of (your specialty), and I was told that department reports to Mr. Balas. Is that correct? Great! Now to better familiarize myself with your department, are there any other departments (functions, sections, regions, etc.) that report to your department? Wonderful! Now I have some specific questions for Mr. Balas. Tell me, when is the best time to try to contact him? Okay, fine! I will be certain to call at that time." (*And be sure to call exactly at the time you said you would!*)

The call to your contact's boss is exactly like the call to the Chief Executive Officer above. And that's it.

Now, in case you are thinking that this process seems pretty lengthy for the information obtained, let me share something with you.

I am going to describe the process of double clutching a truck transmission when shifting to a lower gear. I want you to notice what impression it makes on you while reading through the required steps. First, depress the clutch with your foot. Second, move the gear shift handle to the neutral gear position. Third, release the clutch. Fourth, depress the accelerator approximately one-third to one-half the full travel distance to increase engine RPM's. Fifth, depress the clutch pedal with the foot and move the gear shift handle to the desired lower gear position. Finally, release the clutch pedal and gradually depress the accelerator to achieve the desired vehicle speed.

Sounds pretty lengthy and involved. In reality, it only takes about one-half of one second to do it.

The same principle holds true with the "positive error" process described in this chapter. Though it may seem intricate and involved, it really isn't. It will take you no time at all to get the information you need. This means you are well on your way to another network meeting.

CHAPTER 12

DEALING WITH TELEPHONE RUN-AROUND

How many times has this happened to you? You try to call someone only to find that the person is out of town, away from her desk, in a meeting, unable to come to the phone right now, is not taking any calls at the moment, or just not in? Then the secretary says, "However, I can take your name and number and have her return your call?" At this point, you are wondering, "Should I leave my name and number? After all, this person doesn't even know me. She will probably think I'm a sales person or head hunter. So there will be absolutely no incentive to call me back . . . especially since this is a toll call." So you decide against leaving the information and ask, "When do you expect her?" To which the secretary responds, "I'm really not sure. She has a 10:30 meeting this morning. Maybe if you try calling right after lunch you can reach her then." So you agree to try later and hang up.

At 2:00 P.M. you try again. "Oh, I'm sorry, Mr. Smith. Mrs. Ellis had to leave rather unexpectedly. Apparently something came up that required her immediate attention. May I take your number and have her return your call?" So you figure, "Why not? Two attempts at calling *her* hasn't worked." So you leave your telephone number hoping she will make a concerted effort to return your call first thing in the morning.

On the next day, the morning passes and no call. You wonder, "Should I call her?" No, you conclude, That would be rude. "After all she has *my* number, so there is nothing to keep her from calling me when she has a free moment."

The next day, you return from a networking meeting and find a message that says, "While you were away, Mrs. Ellis called." You quickly look at your watch. Since her call came in only twenty minutes ago, you quickly call her office. "Yes, this is Howard Smith. I'm returning Mrs. Ellis' call." The secretary says, "Oh, yes, Mr. Smith. Mrs. Ellis said to tell you that if you called while she was out of the office that she was sorry that she had missed you and you should try her later. She will be tied up in a management meeting for the rest of the day." Frustration! Frustration! Frustration!

There are no guarantees when it comes to any technique used on the telephone. However, there are always things we can do to increase our chances for a successful outcome, and telephone run-around (or "telephone tag" as it has often been referred to) is no different.

The biggest mistake you can make at this point is to assume the person doesn't want to talk to you. Remember, there is a reason why you are calling this particular person. It is because he or she has hiring authority as well as a whole host of supervisory and/or managerial responsibilities that go along with this authority. This is a busy, responsible person with a very low priority assigned to returning an unknown inquirer's call. Your objective is to be tactfully persistent. Don't stop calling until this person tells you to do so.

Getting the run-around on the telephone can be extremely frustrating. However, here is a word of caution: The last thing you want to do at this point is show even the slightest indication of your frustration. Each attempt to call should be made as though it is the first time you have tried reaching your contact.

So, what can we do to increase our chances of connecting? *Make telephone appointments.*

For example:

*Instead of
doing this:* "Would you please ask her to return my call at (203) 555-1234? I will be in my office all day."

*You might
try this:* "Here is what I can do. I can call back again at 9:30 or if that's not good, I can try her at 11:00. In your judgment, which is best for her? Fine, I will call her again at 11:00 A.M. In the event she is not available at 11:00 A.M., please ask her to suggest an alternative time to call so that I can try again at that time."

OR

This: "I'm in the habit of not making any calls between _____ and _____ so I can receive incoming calls. If she can call me at that time, I will be expecting her call, and this way we won't miss each other."

Here's another variation on the same theme. Let's suppose that the person you are calling is traveling and is not expected to return until the following Monday morning. Stop for a moment and put yourself in his shoes. Most likely, your contact will want to examine the in-basket to determine the volume of work and the various priorities that he or she must assign to each task. This means reading mail, filling out expense reports, getting caught up on projects and meetings, and returning telephone calls . . . all in prioritized order. So for all intents and purposes, your request for a return call would be low in priority at least for the first two days, since your contact will need time to get back in the swing of things. Here's how I would suggest "leaving word" of your call for a returning traveler:

*Speaking
to the
secretary:* "If Mrs. Borgessen will be back on Monday, my

best bet is not to call her until Wednesday, since she'll probably have a lot to do when she gets back. Mr. Merrill, if you could do me a favor and leave a note for her that *I will call her* on Wednesday morning, the 17th, at 10:00 A.M., I would appreciate it. Now, if this is not a good time to call her, please ask her to tell you the best alternative time for me to call. In this way, I can get that information from you and improve my chances of speaking with her."

By setting telephone appointments, you will be reducing the chances of chasing each other around. However, I would like to make one point clear. I am not saying that because *you* have made an appointment, *you* are guaranteed of getting a return call. I am saying that I have tried this technique myself, and it works nicely . . . most of the time.

Ironically, the way I discovered its effectiveness is not something I would wish on anyone. I placed a call to someone who was out at the time, and left a message that I would call back at 10:00 A.M. As it turned out, my contact respected my request. Unfortunately, *I did not live up to my end of the bargain, because I had forgotten about the call and did not call him back until 11:00 A.M.!* I began the conversation by saying, "Good morning, Mr. Gamse. You don't know me. My name is Howard Armstrong. I tried reaching you yesterday but I guess you were out of the office." He said, "Yes, I have a note here that says someone by the name of Howard Armstrong called and would be calling me back at 10:00 A.M." You can imagine my embarrassment. The technique works. Don't make the mistake of proving it to yourself the way I did!

In summary, you can increase your chances of making a connection if you make telephone appointments for either in-coming or out-going calls. Tactful persistence is the order of the day. Remember the story I told you in Chapter 5 about the Vice President of Operations for an outplacement firm who "created" a job for me? We laugh about it now, but it actually took six weeks of persistent calling to make the first connection. That's right, six weeks. And remember, I wound up ultimately conducting *many* seminars for those folks as a result of this persistence.

CHAPTER 13

WHEN YOU JUST DON'T FEEL LIKE MAKING THE CALLS

One of the most important ingredients of successful networking is persistence. You must maintain a steady stream of contacts who will put you in touch with the right people on a regular basis. If, for some reason, there's a lull in your telephone activity, it will result in fewer meetings. You cannot afford to let that happen. Yet, there will be times when you will feel like you just can't get started. How do you overcome that feeling? Here's an idea that continues to work wonders for me.

The magic comes from a little self-talk that says, "I bet you can't make just one!" In other words, I would be willing to bet if you try this simple and not so sophisticated technique that you will experience absolutely no difficulty in making the *second* telephone call (and the third, fourth, etc.). In fact, the technique is so simple, you're probably going to be disappointed when I tell you what it is.

All you have to do is make the first call of the day, an easy one. (See, I told you you'd be disappointed.) So, you say, what do I mean by "an easy one"? Well, I mean you should make the first call of the day to any one of several contacts suggested below. For example, an easy call could be to . . .

*A Person
You've Been
Referred To* Referral calls are always easier to make than blind calls, for obvious reasons. You and your contact have a friend or business associate in common. That little parcel of common ground is a miraculous ice breaker in getting the conversation started.

*A Business
Associate* Talking to someone you know can do wonders to get you started. It should be someone who knows your situation and whose "door is always open." I am not suggesting that you call to waste anyone's time, but rather to make brief contact with someone you are comfortable talking to. Maybe you can share an idea you discovered while in an information meeting with someone else, or perhaps you can call this person to set a date for lunch just to get together.

*Follow-up
Call to a
Previous
Contact* Review your list of previous contacts and look for someone who reacted to your initial call in a friendly and positive manner. You may just want to thank them for the referral they gave you and keep them abreast of what took place during your call to the referral contact. These people are easier to talk to, because you have already broken the ice. They can also serve as a genuine catalyst to get networking activity going.

*Low
Priority
Contact* This could be a company that ranks low on your priority list of calls, because they're outside the industry, organization level, geographic location, specialty or whatever that

you are interested in. What is common to all these contacts is that the pressure is off. That is, there is no liability, if the call doesn't go as planned. Therefore, it's a lot easier to make the call.

I call it magic, but there's really no magic involved. All you have to do is to make that first call. The rest will take care of itself. On any given day, when you are experiencing difficulty in getting started, the first call can be the toughest. By making the first call the easiest one, you will be on your way.

While collecting my thoughts about this chapter, I remembered something that occurred to me while attending a Broadway play in New York. This particular play had been running for quite some time. Despite the fact that I was seeing it for the first time, some of the actors described in the Playbill were said to have made hundreds of appearances in this very play. I couldn't help wondering how those actors and actresses were able to get up there repeatedly and give a performance that to me looked like opening night in terms of its freshness, vitality, and entertainment value.

I concluded that it must be their sheer professionalism. This is determination to give it their all, because that is what the profession requires.

Something else suddenly occurred to me. Acting is a profession full of insecurities. There's never any guarantee about the next job. If I were a Broadway actor, I would be certain to make every performance my best. Who knows, there just might be a producer looking for just the right person for a role or have the perfect role for me to play. Heaven help me if, on that particular day, I just did not feel like I wanted to give it my all!

Guess what? The same philosophy holds true with networking. The one time you "don't feel like doing it" may be the time to give it everything you've got. You see, your next contact might know someone who has just the right opportunity for you.

CHAPTER 14

WHEN YOU MAKE THE CALLS BUT DON'T GET THE MEETINGS

What happens if you can't schedule a meeting?

Let's assume you have a plan. You have a list of contacts to call every day. You have your introductory statement on script. You've even picked up the telephone and called many of them. But one of two things is happening. First, perhaps, you experienced a reasonable number of successes early on. However, as time passed, the ratio of information meetings to the total number of telephone calls declined. Second, maybe you've made several calls but have experienced little or no success in getting information meetings right from the very start. In essence, you're making the effort, yet something is wrong. And, in either case, you're having a tough time determining the source of your difficulty.

In the first situation, your performance is analogous to the professional athlete who has hit upon a slump. It doesn't mean that he is no longer able to "do it" (whatever "it" is). It simply means that something is different. Something has changed.

Since these are two distinctively different situations with the same symptom (no meetings), we are going to take two different approaches to improve your performance.

In the first situation, we're going to improve your performance by *analyzing your successes*. In the second, we are going to examine the process step by step, using a check list. Both methods will force you to draw a comparison between what will bring success and what you are currently doing. However, both methods also require one very important ground rule: Be brutally frank in your assessment of the process you have put together. Let's begin by taking a look at the first guidelines, "analyzing your successes".

In this situation, we're going to assume that your early attempts to obtain information meetings were successful. You were focused, and your approach was centered around one specific specialty. You had put together a script. You also took the time to anticipate the challenges, and you handled them well. You asked for and got the information meetings, and these expanded your network. Then, for some reason, people no longer seemed interested in helping you out. Others would not speak to you. Still, others would not only decline to meet with you but also refused to provide you with any referrals.

By now, you may be asking yourself, "Why would I want to analyze my successes? To me, it seems that the problem can be solved by analyzing my errors instead." The answer to that question is simple expediency. If we can determine what ingredients resulted in success, the chances are that we can be successful again by repeating the successful process. In my twenty plus years of professional experience, I have concluded that the only benefit that comes from analyzing our errors in regard to individual performance is that we become real experts at "how *not* to do it."

The first step in analyzing your successes is to remember the earlier successful calls that you made. What did you do then that you don't do now? Or, what didn't you do then that you *are* doing now? Try to recreate one of those successful dialogues in your mind. Try to imagine every detail of the call. When you discover differences between then and now (regardless of how subtle you think they are), chances are you have discovered the difference between success and failure. For example, perhaps what has changed is not the script or your answers to the challenges, but rather your level of confidence. It stands to reason that if you were successful early on at obtaining information meetings, your confidence was bolstered by your success, and that's good! However, if by some chance your confidence is perceived as complacency, your contact may feel as though he is being processed. In other words, you are too relaxed and too confident. The energy is somewhat subdued and that enthusiastic ring is gone. This is when your contacts feel as if they are calling number 23 out of 25 to be made today. That was not your intention!

Awareness is roughly 75 percent of the solution. Be sensitive to the fact that, because you have been doing this for a while, your approach may be lacking the nervous energy that was once there. Of course, I am not suggesting that you deliberately begin to sound nervous to get that energy back. To the contrary, you should capitalize on your confidence by injecting enthusiasm into your conversation with the expectation that you will be successful once again.

Similarly, because you appear confident over the telephone, you may sound too smooth to your contact. If that's the case, it can be deadly in its effect on your ability to get information meetings. The one thing you don't want your contact to feel is that you are very smooth *because you have been doing this for a long time.* In fact, you may be giving your contact the impression that you are a "professional job hopper." Why would they get that impression? You sound too good! Once again, awareness is probably 75 percent of the solution. Maybe all that is needed is to slow down and put some strategic pauses into your scripted introductory statement.

If you sound like someone in genuine need of assistance in your career search, that's one thing. However, if you are making all those calls, feeling pretty good about it, and coming across with the smoothness of a radio talk show host, the first order of business is to *slow down!* Remember how tentative you were when you first started making your calls? As rough as you thought you sounded, you were probably perceived as someone making a sincere appeal for help. That is not to say that what you are doing now is not sincere. It still is! It's just that your increased level of comfort from making so many calls may now be working against you, and your contact feels as though he is being approached by a pro.

Here is one final suggestion. If you acted on my recommendation to tape some of your earlier calls, play the tapes over now a few times. See if you can detect any differences between the way you conduct your calls now and the way you did before. Listen carefully. The difference could be very subtle, yet may hold the key as to why you are not getting the same reaction from your contacts.

Now, let's take a look at another problem situation. Once again, your attitude is positive, because you are making the calls. But you aren't getting enough meetings. We're going to tackle this situation using a checklist. I want you to examine each process step by step, asking yourself the questions within it. You must be totally honest with yourself when evaluating each step. Otherwise, you're only going to be fooling yourself.

TELEPHONE NETWORKING PROCESS CHECKLIST

1. Are you calling for work or an information meeting?

If you are working on a hidden agenda, *calling in the hope that they will have a job for you,* you are only kidding yourself and setting yourself up for a tremendous disappointment! The chances of your contact having an opportunity in your specific area of expertise at that precise moment is next to none. What you want, as Jack Falvey says, is the opportunity to *be good* in person, unlike the rest of the folks out there who are trying to *look good* on paper. Being good in person does not suggest a performance. It simply means being yourself while presenting your knowledge, skills, and work experience. The getting-the-job stage is part of the interview process, but it must be preceded by the "marketing" stage that is the topic of this book.

2. Are you focused?

Throughout the entire telephone networking process, there are three major areas of focus. These are your specialty, your telephone call objective, and your meeting objective.

Your Specialty

Your approach should be centered around a specific specialty. Anything else, in my opinion, has the look and sound of "trolling" for opportunities. Approach your contact with the theme that this is the opportunity you are researching. Some of my seminar participants approach their contacts by saying, "Who knows, our conversation may lead to my deciding that this is no longer the right career for me to pursue."

If you feel that you will be losing an opportunity because you do not inform your contact of all your experience or the positions you have held, I maintain that your thrust should be specific. The time for revealing multiple skills is during the meeting, not on the telephone. During the meeting, your contact will become aware of your capabilities and will probably consider you quite a find.

Your Telephone Objective

Your primary objective for making the call is to *get a face-to-face meeting with your contact*. Period! The problem, however, is that once you have placed several calls, you become too at ease with the process. This often leads to non-productive small talk. Don't fall into this trap! Look for opportunities to ask for the meeting and then get a commitment.

Your Meeting Objective

Though not an integral part of the telephone call, its importance bears mentioning anyway. Your primary objective during the face-to-face meeting is to *get at least two more names for expanding your network.*

3. Scripting

Putting together a few brief notes on paper and having it in front of you while placing the call can do wonders for the image you are creating.

The importance you placed on saying the right things in your cover letter are no less significant here. The chances are when you sat down to write your first cover letter, you didn't just jot down a few words and then mail it with the attitude, "Let the chips fall where they may." In reality, the chances are very good that you agonized over just about every word, because you felt you had one chance to make a significant impact. Winging it is out! A well thought-out script will have several powerful advantages. These advantages include:

a. Having a prepared statement (or a set of notes) in front of you to significantly reduce any apprehensions you may be experiencing.

b. Ensuring that your introductory statement will have the impact you want, because you will have thought about every word you want to use.

c. Preventing the problem of "going blank."

Here is one last point about scripting. Remember the ground rules. Tell the truth and be yourself. Embellishing the facts can be embarrassing. Trying to come across as someone other than who you are by overworking your sentences or trying to sound "business like" just doesn't work. Speak in conversational sentences within your own personality, and you will do just fine!

4. Anticipation

By taking the time to script what you want to say and thinking about the challenges you may be confronted with, you will be well armed to handle the vast majority of calls you will make.

Here is a list of possible situations you should consider to prepare yourself *ahead of time* for such eventualities:

Would you know what to do if:

- ☐ Instead of giving you the name of your contact, the receptionist puts you directly through to him, and the next thing you hear is your contact's voice saying, "Johnson!"

- ☐ Your contact says, "Well, just send me your resume, and I'll get back to you."

- ☐ The receptionist says, "Are you looking for work?"

- ☐ Your contact says (when speaking of your referrer), "Yeah I know him. He's a real jerk!"

- ☐ Your contact says, "Yeah, I get hundreds of resumes every day."

It's not the answers to the questions that are so difficult. It's the element of surprise that occurs when you had not considered the possibility of being asked that question. Be prepared!

5. Asking for the meeting

Are you asking for the meeting—or are you just having a pleasant conversation? The latter is easy once you are used to the process. In reality, it is a pitfall that can cause you to spin your wheels.

Remember, the time to ask for a meeting is when your contact:

a. asks questions about you.

b. offers a challenge, such as "Why are you out of work?"

c. says something positive about you, your approach, telephone voice, plan of action, the company you used to work for, etc.

In summary, if you have experienced some success or no success at all, one thing is for sure. You are making the effort, which means that your attitude is positive. The problem is somewhere in the process. As long as you make a concerted effort to discover exactly which part of the process is not working for you, you will be on your way to getting those meetings.

CHAPTER 15

PITFALLS

There are several potential trouble spots I should caution you about when you are conducting telephone networking. These pitfalls are varied and easy to overlook. They merit a close examination here.

1. Beware of, "Why don't you tell me a little bit about yourself?" Never allow yourself to be interviewed over the telephone. When you are asked, "Tell me a little about yourself," then do just that. Tell them a little bit . . . just enough to create interest. In about 10–15 seconds, you can give your contact an overview of your accomplishments over the last year to eighteen months. *However, I would not go back any further.* Follow up your "brief commercial message" with, ". . . but of course I was hoping to give you a more detailed description when we meet."

Your contact may have more subtle ways to ease you into an interview. It could begin with an innocent-sounding question like, "Well, what sort of experience have you had as an (your specialty)?" Answer the question, but appeal to your contact by saying, " . . . but of course if I say any more, I will be stealing my own thunder, as I hope you will give me an opportunity to discuss these things in greater detail when we meet."

2. You don't want an interview. You want a meeting.

You may have noticed throughout this book that I always refer to the time that you and your contact get together as *a meeting and not an interview*. Think about it. If you ask for an interview, what does that sound like? To me, it sounds like you want to be interviewed for a job. It's almost as if you have a hidden agenda tied to getting together. Eliminate the word "interview" from your vocabulary when speaking to your contact. (When the time does come to schedule a real, live interview, consider getting a copy of Martin Yate's excellent book, *Knock 'em Dead with Great Answers to Tough Interview Questions*.)

3. Reason or rubber stamp?

Believe me, sounding too good is a very real possibility. Once you've tried the process on for size and tailored it to your own personality, you will begin to sound very polished in no time. There is nothing wrong with the sound of confidence. We would all like to hire people who demonstrate a high level of self confidence. However, if presented with a question or challenge that you have heard many times before, you will be tempted to say to your self, "Piece of cake" and then rattle off a quick answer. When the answers come quickly *and* smoothly, it's time to slow down. Your contact should be left with the impression that he has been hand-picked for this discussion. This perception can evaporate, if you handle their challenges in a hasty manner. In responding to your contact's questions and challenges, pause for a moment. You may even want to paraphrase the question in your own words for the express purpose of slowing things down. Then, answer the question in a poised, confident manner, demonstrating that the answer is coming from reason instead of from a rubber stamp.

4. "It didn't work. Therefore I must have done something wrong."

If you like what you have read so far, you may get the impression that this program is a good one. Suppose, however, that suddenly, for no apparent reason, the process doesn't work. The pitfall here is that since you are implementing a process that makes sense to you, it seems only reasonable to assume that (if carried out correctly) it will always work. And if it doesn't work, "I must have made a mistake somewhere in the process." *Nothing works all the time regardless of how well you follow the guidelines provided.* This is not a disclaimer, it is simply a fact of life. On the other hand, if the *majority* of your efforts prove unsuccessful, *then* I would suggest going back to Chapter 14 to see if something can be done to improve your batting average.

5. Keep trying until they tell you not to call.

There will be times when you will try contacting someone several times only to hear, "I'm sorry, but she is not in right now," or "he's in a meeting," or "I'm afraid she's still away from her desk," or "Oh I'm sorry but he was called away rather unexpectedly," and so on. The pitfall is assuming the contact doesn't want to speak to you. After several unsuccessful attempts to reach your contact, you begin to get the feeling someone is just putting you off or hoping you will get discouraged and finally stop calling. And that's a *big mistake!*

A story I tell my seminar participants concerned my attempts to contact a Vice President of Operations for a fairly large company. For six weeks, I heard nothing but reasons why she could not speak with me. However, no message was ever passed along that I should stop calling or that she was not interested in my offering. Weeks later, I finally connected with this person, and ultimately got the business!

If you are trying to get an appointment with someone who has hiring authority, remember that by virtue of their job description alone, these people are going to be busy. Be patient and keep trying. In fact, a general rule that I use is not to stop calling until they tell me to. And to the best of my recollection for the past years, the people that I called on for the first time have *never* told me to stop calling.

6. "Never count your chickens . . . "

I have seen many people fall victim to the next pitfall despite ample warning. It happens like this. You contact someone through your telephone network (or become aware of an opportunity through some other means). To your delight, they have you speak with a hiring executive within an organization that, frankly, you would love to work for. The meeting goes well. They have you meet other people within their organization and those meetings go well. Everything looks great! It's a good company that has a nice working environment, friendly people, and a great compensation package. It is just what you have been looking for! Here's the pitfall. After a couple positive meetings, you start thinking, "This is it! My efforts have finally paid off. The position is perfect and I bet they're going to make me an offer!" And so what happens? You commit the sin of all networking sins. You decrease your efforts and begin to slack off on your daily contacts for networking meetings.

You can probably imagine the rest of the story. There is no offer, and the let-down is devastating! Now, you've got two problems. First, you did not get an offer, and it will take much effort to recover from the disappointment. Second, it will take twice the effort to gain back the momentum you established before you started talking to these people.

Never stop networking until you have accepted an offer. By continuing to network while a great opportunity surfaces, you will be doing two things in your interest. First, you will continue to be so busy that you won't find yourself thinking about how great the opportunity is. Second, by having a lot more "irons in the fire," the disappointment of not receiving an offer (should that happen to you) will be a lot easier to bear. This is true, since you are currently working on other equally good opportunities!

7. They're nicer at the top!

There will be times when your contact or referral is pretty high up on the corporate ladder. If you are not accustomed to dealing with senior management, the thought of calling this contact might be somewhat intimidating to you. The pitfall is assuming that the higher the person's position is in the organization, the tougher he gets. This just isn't so. The truth of the matter is that the higher up you go, the more willing people seem to be to help. Don't assume that you are going to have a tough time just because they have "Vice President" or "President" next to their names. They may well be some of the nicest people you will deal with while networking.

8. Fear of offending
Occasionally, you will have a meeting with someone that leads to an interview. Upon completion of the interview, you are told that a decision will be made in a week to ten days. At that time, they will contact you with the results of their decision. You should never assume that their sense of urgency is as great as yours. Anything can happen to stall the hiring process past the intended date of the decision. The question now becomes, "Should I call them?" My approach is to take the initiative. I have never heard of anyone who was turned down for a position for assertively following up on an interview. Call them. You have a right to know what is going on. Assuming they do not want you, because the date of the decision has come and gone is a mistake. You can simply call the hiring decision maker and say, "Mr. X, I thought I would call to determine where you are in your decision for the position of (your specialty)." The chances are that you will be perceived as proactive. Once again, you will set yourself apart from the other applicants who are still sitting at home, waiting for the letter that never arrives.

9. Not keeping your hard-won network alive . . . after you have landed the position.
Believe it or not, the last pitfall occurs *after* you have accepted a position. The American economy is volatile at best. Daily press reports tell of mergers, acquisition, joint ventures, and takeovers. These almost always seem to result in

reorganizations, down-sizings, and reductions in force. Phrases, such as "overhead," "redundancy," and "business decision" are often used in the difficult process of eliminating human resources to assure the organization's survival. I have worked for a company that was bought and sold three times. I have also been outplaced twice and fired once. I have concluded that God and I are the principals who determine what I do and where I work.

The old idea of getting an education, being hired by a good company, working hard, and retiring comfortably is exactly that . . . old! Business decisions go far beyond our dreams, goals, intentions, and desires for our families and ourselves. A "good" company today is no longer a "safe bet" when it comes to security. You must determine what will happen to you. Working hard is no guarantee of security either. I was working very hard during those times, when I was "selected" for outplacement. Some business decisions generally do not contain effort, experience, or excellence ratings to determine who goes and who stays.

There is still a strong possibility that you may link up with an organization that will keep you on until *you* decide to leave. If you don't, the good news is that you possess a step-by-step process that can lessen the blow of another business decision that effects you. Not only do you have the process, but you also have something else. No one can put a price tag on the value of this, and this is *your network*! So what is the pitfall? *It is failing to keep your network alive while you are gainfully employed!*

You have worked very hard to build your network. You've seen what it can do for you. Keep it alive and strong with an occasional telephone call, birthday card, hand-written note (or letter), or holiday greeting card. You may want to consider sending out a newsletter to your network. In this newsletter, you could inform them of which company you decided to go with and then send out an update from time to time. Be sure to make a personal phone contact at least once every six months. If there are a lot of people to contact, use a staggered schedule. By doing so, you won't have so many calls to make all at once. If you find that members of your network have moved on to other companies, this is better for you. Each time one of your contacts makes a move, this becomes an automatic network expansion because of the associations he will be making within his new organization.

❑   ❑   ❑

Though some of these pitfalls appear on the surface to be doomsday news, they are not intended to be. These pitfalls are the result of experiences that I and many of my seminar participants have had, and are mentioned here in the hope that you will benefit from them.

CHAPTER 16

QUESTIONS, COMMENTS, OR CONCERNS

This chapter contains several questions I am asked, particularly in follow-up sessions after seminar participants have had an opportunity to try these techniques for themselves. Here are some of these questions:

If the telephone is such a great tool in helping me to find a job, why aren't more people encouraged to use it?

At least one "Job Hunting" book says that telephone networking is strictly for the "tough-skinned" individual. In other words, telephone networking is reserved only for the most assertive, and I strongly disagree with this! Successful use of the telephone has nothing to do with assertiveness, and everything to do with being prepared! The major cause of "phonaphobia" is fear of the unknown. If the caller does not have a structured approach, he will, in all likelihood, realize his worst fears. On the other hand, a successful outcome will result from a planned approach. This approach includes the following components:

- ❑ A crystal clear idea of the position being sought.
- ❑ A specific calling objective (to get a face-to-face meeting).

- A carefully written and thoroughly rehearsed introductory statement about why you are calling.
- A thorough review of likely questions and challenges.
- A sincere request to meet with someone who has the potential to help you expand your network and improve your job hunting strategy.

You don't seem too hot on resumes. Shouldn't that be the major thrust of our call? Seems to me it would make more sense to send a resume first, then make a follow up telephone call. At least, the follow up is a perfect excuse to call.
I believe resumes can play an important role in the overall process. My feeling is that resumes should help the hiring decision-maker *confirm* his decision, as opposed to ruling someone out as a result of one or two details that separate the candidate from the job specification. Your resume is not you! *You* are you. And the only way your contact will find out what you are really all about is by meeting you face to face. If you are asked to send a resume, I suggest you mention that you had fully intended to bring an updated version with you when you meet. If you use your resume as your primary means of contact, you are a non-person. When you pick up the telephone and call them, you become a human being. Resumes don't get hired—people do!

I still think it's a good idea to send some form of correspondence first and then follow up with a call.
If you feel more comfortable with a mailing as your first step, I recommend that you send an "accomplishment letter." This is a brief "commercial message" describing your accomplishments over the last year to eighteen months. You should also include a statement to the effect that you will be following up with a telephone call at a later time. The letter will serve to pique your contact's interest, while leaving the details of your experience as further ammunition for the meeting.

I sent out a lot of resumes and cover letters. One of my contacts said he would get back to me, but never did. That was about a month ago. Should I bother to contact him since it was so long ago, or should I drop it?

By all means, give him a call. Hiring decisions can be stalled for many reasons. Never assume that the reason they have not gotten back to you is that they have made a decision in favor of someone else. Just call and say something like, "I was going through my follow-up file and noticed that it was time to give you another call. Can you give me an update on where I stand?" Notice that you are not apologizing for not contacting them. You are also not berating them for neglecting you. Your question is matter-of-fact with the ring of "business as usual."

How do I know if the contact I have been given is "qualified"?

I assume by "qualified", you mean someone who has hiring authority. And there's the rub. In my judgment all leads are qualified. Even if they do not have the authority to hire people, it's *who they know* that counts. In the last chapter of this book, I present a college newsletter article, written by a graduate who is a living model of how to network. This author winds up taking a job that was posted in the classified ads. However, he was made aware of the ad by an "unqualified contact!"

Are you suggesting that I stop sending resumes and cover letters as a way of establishing market presence and replace that with telephone networking?

I'm suggesting that if you want to compress the time it takes to find the right opportunity by 25 percent to 75 percent, telephone networking has this potential. I'm suggesting that if you've tried broadcast mailings and are disappointed with the results, you should do as Rosita Perez does. Rosita is a member of the National Speaker's Association, she says, "Stop following the yellow brick road when it only leads to more yellow bricks!"

I don't buy into the idea that we are calling for "information meetings!" We are looking for jobs, and our contact knows it. I thing we're just kidding ourselves by going through the charade of asking for an information meeting!

If *you* feel that *you* are calling for work, then *it is* a charade. Further, if you *are* calling in hopes of locating a position at the point of contact, I'm afraid that law of averages is against you. Your chances of locating an opening in your particular field of expertise when you call is slim, and that's the good news! Once you tell your contact that *you know the chances of the company having an open position is next to none,* the barriers come crashing down, and this person will in all likelihood only be too glad to help.

I am looking at opportunities on the west coast. Since I'm on the east coast, how do I conduct my network calls? Obviously I can't be setting up information meetings, since the opportunities I'm looking for are thousands of miles away.

That's a tough one. If you are currently working with an out-placement firm that has offices nationwide, you might contact one of their offices on the west coast and ask for their advice. Usually they will offer the same support they provide on the local level. If you are interested in larger companies, you might also try to find local contacts in subsidiaries who would be willing to meet with you briefly. This contact can in turn recommend someone in his company on the west coast to contact for more leads. One of my seminar participants planned a one-week trip to the west coast, but he was very careful to do his homework *before* he left. He called several companies in California, stating that he was in the process of researching opportunities on the west coast. During the conversation, he stated that he was planning to meet with several companies during the week of (X) and said, "I would like an opportunity to meet with you as well to learn as much as I can before committing myself to a move." His approach was so successful that he planned a second trip for more networking.

I want to start telephone networking, but I'm really not sure what I want to do. How should I approach my contacts?

I strongly recommend that you avoid contacting anyone until you have decided what you want to do. Set a comfortable goal for yourself that says, "By (X date), I will have committed to a specific career endeavor." Next, do everything in your power to achieve that goal on or before the date to which you committed. The problem with being undecided is if you begin to contact people with a vague or nebulous approach, they will sense your lack of commitment. As a result, they will not take you seriously. You must be focused when making those calls.

A few days ago, a friend who is a software engineer, told me she was given offers by two companies. She said that I should contact the company she turned down and apply for the position. My question is, how should I approach the hiring company for consideration?

First, I would find out why your friend turned the offer down at this company. I realize that she can only work for one of the companies, but there must be some reason why she chose one over the other. Now, let's assume that her reasons for not selecting the company that interests you are legitimate (e.g., the commute would be too far for her but not for you). In this case, since you know the opportunity exists, I would take a direct approach and go for it! Simply get the name of the hiring executive from your friend. Call that person and say something like, "Good morning, Mr. X! My name is (your name), and my purpose in calling is that I learned that you are in the process of hiring software engineers. Having functioned as a software engineer over the past (X amount of time), I would like to have the opportunity to present myself as a potential candidate for the position." If they are still looking, you will probably be well received. As a qualified candidate, you may be saving them headhunter fees.

I don't believe answering a classified ad under the guise of an "information meeting" will work. What are your thoughts?
I agree! Answering an ad is an entirely different situation. As in the case above, state your interest in the opportunity and proceed accordingly. Telephone networking is extremely effective in uncovering the hidden job market, as opposed to following up opportunities.

Okay, let's assume that my contact agrees to meet with me. Since this is an "information meeting," what kind of information should I try to get?
The agenda is really yours to determine. Keep in mind that your primary objective is to get at least two names from your contact. Do that first by giving your contact a brief overview of your work experience emphasizing your accomplishments. A word of caution: don't go back any further than three years unless asked to do so. Next, I would ask the following questions:

1. How would you describe a successful candidate for the position of (your specialty)?

2. In your opinion, why is it that some people don't "make it" in the position of (your specialty)?

3. What would you say is the criteria for success for someone who has recently been hired on as a (your specialty)?

4. This next question comes from Jack Falvey's book, entitled *What's Next? Career Strategies After 35* (Another great book on careers): "If you were in my position, what would you do?"

5. Is there anything else you feel I should be aware of in my search?

6. Mr. X, I have made it my personal challenge to get at least two names from every person I meet with. Who can you recommend?

When the meeting is over, write a thank-you note on your personalized stationery. A personal hand-written note is the ultimate appreciative touch. It demonstrates to your contact that you are grateful the time he spent with you, and you are extending an effort on your part to return the favor, instead of sending a form letter requiring only a signature.

I always have a problem ending the telephone conversation. How can I end the conversation crisply while at the same time being diplomatic about it?

Assuming you are successful in getting a commitment for a meeting, simply say something like, "Wonderful Ms. Jones! I appreciate the opportunity to meet with you next week. Now, before I hang up, let me review the details of our meeting . . . ."

If you are unsuccessful in getting an appointment, you might appeal to the contact's spirit of assistance by saying something like, "Well, before I hang up, Mr. Smith, I've made it my personal challenge to get at least two names from everyone I speak with to expand my network. Would you be able to help me out in *that* regard?"

All you are doing in either case is letting the contact know that you are about to end the conversation. However, before you do, you would like to take a moment to review the details or perhaps ask the contact a question. The last step is very simple. You would say something like, "Well, Ms. Jones, you've been very helpful. Thank you very much, and I hope you have a good day. Good bye!" or, "Ms. Jones, I want to thank you for taking time out of your busy day to speak with me, and I look forward to meeting with you on Wednesday. Good bye!"

Suppose my contact is not in. What would be wrong with saying, "It's a personal matter," when the secretary asks what the call is about?

My response to this is based largely on my own experience. There were many times when I would return to my office, and one or two telephone messages would be waiting for me on my desk. From time to time, I would receive a call from someone whose name I did not recognize. In the section where the pink note says, "Message", the word "personal" was written. Each time I returned one of these calls, it was always (but always) an executive search firm or placement service of some sort. Obviously, it didn't take long to figure out the nature of the call each time I got one of these notes with "personal" written on it.

Rather than trying to be creative about the message you leave when the contact is not in, I believe using the technique provided in Chapter 12 is the best way to handle this situation.

What if I don't feel like doing anything? I'm not just talking about getting the first call made. I'm saying I just don't feel like doing anything at all, let alone making telephone calls.

This question does not pertain to telephone networking itself. However, I feel it is important enough to deal with here, since I think I understand what is happening. What you are experiencing is certainly not "phonaphobia." Every so often I had those days too. This was especially true when I wondered where the money was going to come from to make those mortgage payments. We all get depressed from time to time. The danger with depression is that it can paralyze you. I don't mean physical paralysis. I mean it affects our attitude in such a way that we just shut down. We don't work. We don't do anything. We just sit around and worry. This is both unproductive and unhealthy. Remember, networking requires a continuous effort to realize its potential. If you shut down, you will lose the momentum that you have worked so hard to generate.

As I have said, feeling down some days is perfectly normal. However, you should be aware that a string of such days, ranging from ten days to two weeks, can signal a serious emotional problem. Techniques for dealing with this degree of depression are beyond the scope of this book and can best be dealt with through counseling.

I'll tell you about a little trick I use whenever I become unproductive for whatever reason. When I have reached the point to where I feel like shutting down, the first order of business is activity. Any kind of activity is fine, just as long as I am doing something to keep my mind occupied. To do this, I always keep a list of what I call "No-Brainers". No-Brainer's are activities that I can carry out that require little or no thinking. These are the kinds of things you always say "you're going to do but never have the time for". For example, the list on my desk right now tells me to cull the files, clean and organize my desk, pick up a toner cartridge for the copier at the office supply store, collate seminar handouts, etc. Once I get involved in one of these tasks, it takes my mind off my thoughts just long enough to snap out of whatever troubles me.

Give it a try. Then make some calls!

CHAPTER 17

A REAL-WORLD MODEL OF SUCCESSFUL NETWORKING

"If you think you can, or if you think you can't,
in either case, you're probably right!"
— *Henry Ford*

Now that you have had an opportunity to discover the successful elements of telephone networking, I would like to introduce you to Chris Mellen. He is a 1985 graduate of McGill University, in Montreal, Canada. In 1987, Chris wrote an article in the "McGill News" entitled " . . . it's who you know." This article was so powerful and impressive that it appeared in the *Wall Street Journal's National Business Employment Weekly*.

The article describes how Chris effectively implemented a telephone networking campaign to find the right career opportunity for him. When you read his article, keep in mind that he had no prior work experience to speak of. All he had was an undergraduate degree from a reputable Canadian University, an awareness of the power of networking, and a focused plan of attack. The article is presented in this chapter with permission from the author.

❑   ❑   ❑

In April 1985, my studies at McGill were about to end. The next semester would bring on the real world, and I knew only that after a summer of travel, I wanted to work in the Boston area. But with a B.A. specializing in finance and human resource management, I didn't know exactly what I was looking for. The challenge of the "Job Search" was facing me square on—how was I going to conquer it?

My first attempt left me pretty beaten up: I sent out twenty resumes and cover letters to prospective employers, most resulting in the usual "we'll keep you on file" responses. I answered ads, but there were no bites. Yet by November, I had a job with the State Street Bank & Trust Company in Boston and a large list of professional contacts, all of whom I made while searching for employment. Along the way, I also learned that looking for work need not be a hit-and-miss proposition.

I found two methods of approaching the job search. One is to rely on external factors, by answering advertisements or applying through employment agencies. The other is to decide what field or organization interests you and use the networking contacts made through interviews to pursue employment. One can use both techniques. In fact, my job came through a contact who told me of an advertised position.

The combination of "informational interviewing" and networking is an effective way to job-hunt. The purpose of an informational interview is not to ask for employment but to gather information, improve your interview skills, and make contacts. While a job offer may indeed come up, your objective is this face-to-face meeting. An executive once told me, "Contacts are everything. Who you know will get you ahead of hundreds of resumes." And there is no better way to find out about a company or field than talking with an individual therein.

During the interview ask for additional names, each one to be added to a list or chart that organizes the growing number of contacts. Keep in touch—thank them for their time and inform them of subsequent meetings with their references. Ask for their opinion on job offers, and let them know how it is going once gainfully employed. Jack Falvey, author of *After College: The Business of Getting Jobs* says:

> "[You] may find it hard to believe that some senior management types would clear their calendars for an hour or two just to talk to a student, but they do it all the time. Take advantage of this willingness."

I started my search by asking friends and relatives to set up meetings with people in their companies, which resulted in a few informational and formal interviews as well as two job offers. Neither was interesting, so I searched on.

Needing another source of contacts, I decided to meet with McGill alumni employed in the Boston area. I returned to my alma mater in Montreal and met with the Director of the Graduates' Society, who recommended alumni contacts and discussed job-search strategy with me. Armed with a few more names, I returned to Boston ready to continue networking.

I was certainly not impressive in all my conversations. Interviews take practice, but the point of the process is to learn and improve. Through networking, I was able to arrange interviews with several "senior management types." McGill was not my only source of contacts, but it led to 27 interviews, one of which indirectly led to my present job. Toward the end of my job search, I met 15 people in one week! The networking process can start anywhere with just one reference. Ask each contact for at least two names, meet with them, and the process will snowball. The sheer volume of contacts will almost certainly open up all sorts of possibilities, bring job offers, and provide useful and interesting information.

You are presently, as Falvey puts it, "self-employed with a deferred income." If you work at it full-time, your chances of finding your ideal job will be greater—and you will enjoy getting there. So, if you are in a dilemma on how to go about looking for a job, consider this method. Contacts are everything. It may take some time and much effort, but you must realize that it is *your* job to find a job.

❏   ❏   ❏

HOW DID WE DO IT?

(For those curious about the anecdote at the beginning of Chapter 11.)

We simply did a time and distance calculation. At 120 knots airspeed, you cover 200 feet per second over the ground. We knew the airstrip length. So, we simply flew over the runway, started our stop watch at the beginning of the runway, and stopped it at the end. We multiplied the number of seconds it took to traverse the entire length of the runway by 200 feet and compared the result of the published airstrip length. They matched. There was enough difference between the two airstrip lengths that we could easily determine the difference through this procedure.

Index